PRAISE FOR

THE MARY YEARS

An ekphrasis, an homage, a recuperation of a retrospectively subversive feminist icon, and a deft cultural critique of a 1970s classic television show, Julie Marie Wade's *The Mary Years* is also a delightful and incredibly moving memoir, read entirely through the lens of *The Mary Tyler Moore Show*. *The Mary Years* chronicles Wade's coming of age into independence, into feminism, into coming out as a lesbian and forming an artistic identity as a writer—while overcoming incredible sociocultural and familial pressures to live a life in compliance with conservative political, religious, and heteronormative values. Dazzlingly innovative and shape-shiftingly fluid in form, this memoir is in many ways a love letter to female role models, mentors, friends, and lovers—particularly the ones that light up pathways outside the obligatory confines of limiting and restrictive futures, the ones that illuminate alternate ways of making sense of one's life. Funny, smart, and occasionally heartbreaking, this wonderful memoir has the fierce torque and iconic joy of a bright homemade tam-o-shanter spiraling up into a cold, winter sky.

—LEE ANN RORIPAUGH,
AUTHOR OF *TSUNAMI VS. THE FUKUSHIMA 50*

MORE PRAISE:

Who knew Our Lady of the Tam Toss, '70s icon Mary Richards, would provide the perfect bridge from a strict '50s-values Catholic upbringing for a queer '90s teen? In this unique memoir strung from lyric moments like beads on a rosary, Wade writes her own tender credo—part filmography, part hagiography, part coming-of-age coming-out story—of what it means to be a modern woman. To do so, she looks backward to look forward, a runner—running not *from* but *to*—who prays, *Thank God for re-runs.*

—Heidi Czerwiec,
AUTHOR of **Fluid States**

What an enchanting memoir. You don't have to be a fan of *The Mary Tyler Moore Show*—or even know what it is—to be captivated by this funny, sad, inspiring journey of a clear-sighted woman for whom a fictional character is a guide for navigating life's very real challenges. For *MTM* fans, of course, Julie Marie Wade's book is a not-to-be-missed treat.

—Clifford Thompson,
AUTHOR of **What It Is: Race, Family, and One Thinking Black Man's Blues**

When life doesn't give you the models you need, find them in fiction. "We become ourselves through other people after all," writes Julie Marie Wade at the beginning and end of her nonfiction novella *The Mary Years*. Wade's tam-throwing Dante is Mary Richards of *The Mary Tyler Moore Show*—a scripted character who leads the author out of the many deadlier scripts written for her at birth. Rich in comedic timing and nimbly cinematic, *The Mary Years'* infectious charm never obscures the real pathos of working through homophobia, estrangement, and growing out of as well as into. Reading these pages made me want to make JMW my own MTM.

—SUSANNE PAOLA ANTONETTA,
AUTHOR OF **THE TERRIBLE UNLIKELIHOOD OF OUR BEING HERE**

THE MARY YEARS

THE WINNER OF THE 2023
CLAY REYNOLDS NOVELLA PRIZE

Julie Marie Wade
The Mary Years

SELECTED BY MICHAEL MARTONE

*Established in 2001: The Clay Reynolds Novella Prize
highlights one book a year that excels in the novella form.*

2022 WINNER:

Jane V. Blunschi, *Mon Dieu, Love*
Selected by Renee Gladman

2021 WINNER:

Deirdre Danklin, *Catastrophe*
Selected by Leslie Jill Patterson

PAST WINNERS:*

Cecilia Pinto, *Imagine the Dog*
Dylan Fisher, *The Loneliest Band in France*
Patrick Stockwell, *The Light Here Changes Everything*

*See the complete list of winners & purchase their books on our website:
texasreviewpress.org

THE MARY YEARS
THE MARY YEARS
THE MARY YEARS
THE MARY YEARS
THE MARY YEARS
THE MARY YEARS
THE MARY YEARS
THE MARY YEARS
THE MARY YEARS
THE MARY YEARS
THE MARY YEARS
THE MARY YEARS

JULIE MARIE WADE

★trp
TRP: The University Press of SHSU
Huntsville, Texas 77341

Cataloging-in-Publication Data

Names: Wade, Julie Marie, author.

Title: The Mary years : a novella / Julie Marie Wade.

Description: First edition. | Huntsville : TRP: The University Press of SHSU, [2024] | "Winner of The 2023 Clay Reynolds Novella Prize, selected by Michael Martone."

Identifiers: LCCN 2024009257 (print) | LCCN 2024009258 (ebook) | ISBN 9781680033885 (paperback) | ISBN 9781680033892 (ebook)

Subjects: LCSH: Wade, Julie Marie. | Childhood and youth. | Mary Tyler Moore show (Television program) | Women authors, American—21st century—Biography. | Authors, American—21st century—Biography. | Women television personalities—United States—Influence. | LCGFT: Autobiographies. | Creative nonfiction. | Novellas. | Experimental fiction.

Classification: LCC PS3623.A345 M37 2024 (print) | LCC PS3623.A345 (ebook) | DDC 813/.6—dc23/eng/20240311

LC record available at https://lccn.loc.gov/2024009257

LC ebook record available at https://lccn.loc.gov/2024009258

FIRST EDITION

Cover & interior design by PJ Carlisle

Author photo & JMW logo: Kim Striegel

Printed and bound in the United States of America

TRP: The University Press of SHSU

Huntsville, Texas 77341

texasreviewpress.org

For ADG & MTM

CONTENTS CONTENTS CONTENTS CONTENTS CONTENTS CONTENTS

opening credits

fauntlee hills was my roseburg

lamonts might have been my wjm

pittsburgh was my minneapolis

miami is my tipperary

closing credits

OPENING CREDITS

A name is a door, which someone can leave open, can prop ajar.
Credits are called credits for a reason.
We become ourselves through other people after all.

OPENING CREDITS

She isn't smiling when it begins. This is important to remember. Her eyes are wide, watchful, and the way she touches her tongue to the roof of her mouth suggests she may be staving off tears. The road ahead unfolds toward the city, two cities—*twins*—and she must choose between them. *Make the right choice, Mary.* One city already has a saint. She will become patron of the other. *Saint Mary of Minneapolis.* Her eyes follow the road, follow the exit signs, but her mind is faraway, is flashing back to Roseburg. This is important to remember. The past is always with us, no matter who we are. They threw a party for her—the co-workers at her last job, her friends. We never learn much about that before-life—though we know Mary must have been loved—*Past's Prologue: "Past is [always] prologue," Mary. On CBS in the '70s as much as in Shakespeare's time.* This is important to remember. There's a sign that reads: **GOOD LUCK MARY**, but she won't need it. She has her work ethic, her practicality, and her pluck. Someone uncorks a bottle of champagne. Red roses, a parting gift, resemble Miss America's bouquet. And Mary is our Miss America all grown-up, isn't she, or at least our Miss American Midwest? There's joy in the flashback and sadness, too, but good-bye is just the shadow of hello. This is important to remember. Mary drives a Mustang after all, hinting at the wild horse within. When we see her next, she's walking, a woman alone in winter, no man steering her by the elbow or warming her with his embrace. *Saint Mary of Perambulation.* It's cold, but she's not daunted by the weather. She strides bare-legged in her knee-high boots, her knee-length coat. She carries her groceries home from the store, a certain spring in her step, a loaf of bread bouncing on top of her brown paper bag. Mary is beginning to smile now, to feel herself part of something larger, subsumed in the corner crowd. She wears a tam or tammy hat, which is a women's variant of the tam-o'-shanter worn by men. Mary is like this—pleasant and appropriate but slyly subversive too. *Our Lady of Surprises. Our Lady of More Than What She Seems.* Not the type to draw attention to herself, it takes an extraordinary surge (*this independence! this freedom at last!*) to prompt the twirl, the tossing of her tam into the air. An older woman looks on, envious or admiring or perhaps recalling a day when she did the same. *Saint Mary of Maybes. Saint Mary of Anything-Is-Possible-Now.* We at home have crossed ourselves. We genuflect by screen-glow. We will follow wherever she goes, *Our Lady of the Smile.*

TiME CAPSULE / SNOW GLOBE

You must have seen it before: the blue screen flickering for just a moment: part "Test of the Emergency Broadcast System," part slice of sky through a sunroof window. Then the splitting—eleven iterations of the same woman's name stretched across the screen like rainbow streamers. Is this a celebration, an invocation, both?

You must have heard it too: single glimmer of sound announcing the spectrum of letters and colors to follow. Almost a doorbell. But instead of Avon, *Mary calling!*

Whenever I heard this sound—more urgent than a playground whistle, or a pistol fired at the start of a race—I sprinted toward the kitchen. There I propped my elbows on a placemat, cupped my face with my hands, embraced the bad posture of peering. I leaned so close to the TV I could have kissed our heroine on her grainy cheek, squatted beside her on the passenger seat. For all my life thereafter, I wanted to ride shotgun to that story.

The square brown Magnavox lurked in a corner, balanced on a stack of wicker drawers. There was no remote, just a row of leaden buttons on the base, a simple two-pronged cord that plugged directly into the wall. As habit turned to ritual, my father rigged a VCR so I could tape episodes of *Mary Tyler Moore*. My research at the library revealed there were 168 of them—discrete and intertwining plotlines that informed one another by accretion. The larger arc featured a few essential characters, traced their relationships over seven years.

I catalogued these episodes lovingly, one by one, on long sheets of yellow legal paper. I deleted any duplicate recordings and did my best to edit out commercials. Each six-hour tape held exactly twelve shows without shearing the credits from either end. I worked the math by hand. There is a scrap that shows this. Fourteen tapes were needed to accommodate everything, to make the capsule inviolable, complete.

Eventually, the TV and VCR moved into my bedroom, and later my college dorm, and later still, my first apartment. At some point my mother said I could have the drawers, too, where I stored the tapes as centerpiece of a growing compendium. Was it fitting to say a shrine? I owned an unauthorized biography of Mary Tyler Moore called *The Woman Behind the Smile*; an autobiography I much preferred called *After All*; a number of *TV Guides* where members of the cast had graced the cover; collages I made as still-life complements to their moving stories; a photostat of my 54-page, hand-written fan letter, mailed to MTM's studio address in California; and the crowning glory—an autographed copy of the *Chuckles Bites the Dust* script, which the secretary of my junior high had lifted from a charity auction and presented to me in secret. My love for Mary was already legendary. And though I felt a twinge of guilt about the money they could have raised with that script, I never felt guilty enough to renounce such a grail. The holiness of my hoarding had become indisputable by then.

Those vintage technologies met their fate in a Goodwill donation pile circa 2004. The drawers, splintering for years under their weight, were patched often but collapsed long before. A laptop with a disc drive replaced the ancient television, and seven sleek DVD cases—ordered by season, delivered by Amazon, replete with "Easter eggs" (hidden rewards for fans, extra footage, bonus features)—supplanted my Hefty bag of clunky black cartridges with their unspooling film, which (too many times) I had spun back with a pencil tip pushed into the grooves of their slow-turning wheels. The rest of the archive, of course, I kept.

But I'm getting ahead of myself—a self who has always lagged behind, time-warped and re-wound, a student of perpetual syndication. In 1992 other pre-teens in suburban Seattle donned flannel shirts and Doc Martens, cranked up the volume on their Pearl Jam albums, and staked personal and regional claims to the tortured genius of Kurt Cobain. They rode with older friends and siblings in weathered Aerostars to outdoor concerts at The Gorge. They watched movies like *Singles* and *Reality Bites*, wore fingerless gloves while smoking clove cigarettes, pierced their lips, and cut their hair at jagged angles.

Maybe I was always older, a thirty-something ready for work in a newsroom. Or maybe I was always younger and didn't know how to rebel. Certainly, it didn't help that my parents taught me to fear the world outside our windows—to look back as if I were still strapped in my car seat, the view tilted toward the bygone, a re-run of where we had already been.

"*Nick at Nite* is a Godsend!" my mother exclaimed when the network launched in 1985. I was six at the time, faddish for wanting a future all mine, selfish for refusing to share. *Nick at Nite* proved a friendly retro-prophet. *Nick at Nite* offered an easy route to reform. After all, I was still a girl who had no idea what MTV was, who had never so much as glimpsed a music video. For me, Madonna was Christ's mother only, Michael Jackson just an ordinary schoolboy's name.

Can you spot me there, inside that snow globe, an only child who excelled only at being "Linda's daughter" and "Bill's daughter," with no idea yet how she should claim herself? And would she, in doing so, somehow contradict them both, besmirch the good name they had given her?

Speaking of names:

ONCE UPON A TIME there was a girl named
Mary Moore who often appeared uncredited in
bit movie parts and TV commercials. Julie
Wade understood how it felt to be such a girl.
She was starring uncredited in her own life
story. One day the aspiring actress decided
she needed to distinguish herself with a memorable middle name. She took her father's—the
"Tyler" from George Tyler Moore—which Julie
Wade admired because it struck a chord of
pleasing androgyny. More girls should embrace
the boys in them, she thought, the way Moore
did, and smiled at the pun.

Although Julie could not see the boy in Mary,
she knew he was there, shadowing her first name
like the fletching on an arrow. And it was not
long before Mary Tyler Moore made her three-
named debut in a sitcom. Granted, the sitcom
bore someone else's name—a man, similarly
tripartite, called Dick Van Dyke—but perhaps
that, too, was part of the premonition, her own
eponymous story on the horizon.

Julie Wade stopped to consider the formal
nameplate on her bedroom door. Until this time,
she had only been called "Julie Marie Wade" as
a harbinger of trouble. Until this time, she
had only written her first and last, her given
and sur, on the upper-left corners of her papers
at school. Now she wondered what would happen
if she resolved to occupy more space—to fill
herself in, to flesh herself out, the way Mary.
Tyler Moore had done—and in so doing, to move

(6)

toward a feature role in the narrative already
underway.

Shake that snow globe a few times now. Can you
see me at twelve, going on thirteen, my head
bowed resolutely over the blank page? No, I am
not praying. The snow is not even snow but paper
I have torn up, confetti I have made of my own
mistakes. Is this celebration, invocation, both?
It is hard to say. I write Mary Tyler Moore in
my ledger, then count the letters that add up to
fourteen. On the line below, I write Julie Marie
Wade and count again. These letters also add up
to fourteen. I blink at them, hard, at their
mystical symmetry:

MARY TYLER MOORE
JULIE MARIE WADE

We are both three names now, five syllables,
fourteen letters. Mary and I occupy the same
space on the page. I begin to chant us, as if
I am casting a spell. For all my life thereafter, I will make my mark this way—claiming
everything, I resolve, sparing nothing.
And I will recall the way the camera zoomed,
swift and bird-like, through the upper-left
corner of the Ⓜ in her name, before swelling
to full-sized picture again. There is Mary,
behind the wheel; there is Julie, unseen but
present beside her.

faunTlee hills was my roseburg

pilot episode

DIRECTOR'S NOTE: Sometimes it is not enough to watch Mary's life unfold on television. I read the world she gave me like a map—a merry atlas, if you will—looking for points of intersection in our experiences and plotting coordinates where they do not at first appear.

When I say I come from a snow globe, this is no exaggeration. Fauntlee Hills was built on a bluff overlooking the sea during the early 1950s. Before then those hills were wooded, unsettled. To the east Seattle loomed, like a great silver star of culture and commerce. It beckoned to some; others, it drove away.

Of the families seeking a quieter life—call it solace if you like, call it isolation—the Wade family moved among them. My grandparents belonged to the first wave of new inhabitants, purchasing their house in 1953. Grandma June still lived in that house four decades later. My father came of age there; his sister Linda too. Then he married my mother and moved into another house just like it, just around the corner. And when my parents spoke to me of the future at all, it looked so much like the present, which looked so much like the past, they fused together into a single mural: red-brick; mid-century floor plans; clean-swept carports; flower boxes effervescing with petunias and begonias and geraniums; picture windows with heavy curtains to modulate the light; and peepholes, naturally, on every sturdy door. My parents promised that I would marry one day and move into a house like theirs, a house just around the corner.

I began to wonder how the neighborhood of Fauntlee Hills—small and pretty and hermetically sealed—compared in size and style and homogeneity to the place that gave rise to Mary Richards: *Roseburg*, a fictional town in the real state of Minnesota. More than one person has told me that I seem like I come from a fictional town. Sometimes I believe them.

In my early world we were not used to people moving in, people from the outside, people who had lived somewhere else before. Everyone stayed. Everyone was old. Most of the neighbors were retired by then, so they made a life out of watching, keeping tabs. Remember those peepholes and picture windows? It was a hard place to trespass without getting caught, which is probably why I longed for the thrill of sleuthing. But I was "June Wade's granddaughter" after all, so some people made exceptions for me. They, quite literally, looked the other way as I traipsed through their gardens, crouched inside their tool sheds, hunkered down inside their window wells and rhododendron bushes.

Then Edna Kaufman died. Then Jim Kaufman couldn't take care of himself anymore. Then their children came, who were also old. They cleaned the house, drained the wishing well, took the wind chimes out of the trees. Clearly, they didn't understand whimsy. When they left for good, a FOR SALE sign stood in the yard on two white pickets. I had never seen pickets that weren't part of a fence before, and I had never seen a FOR SALE sign either—not in real life, only on television.

I was playing jacks on my grandmother's drive or picking weeds for pay from her parking strip. I might even have been dangling from one of her flowering trees. But I remember most vividly the day a young blond woman in a dark blazer and paisley skirt parked her Toyota by the curb, wheels turned in just so. The FOR SALE sign wore a sash that read SOLD. The woman took it down. She tried to pull the whole structure out of the ground, but it stuck like a stubborn tooth, and I took her efforts as my entrance cue.

"Hi!" I said, "I'm Julie," in my sitcom-friendly way. "Do you live here now?"

She smiled, and her glasses slipped down on her nose. "Yes. I'm Linda, and as a matter of fact, I do."

"That's my mom's name, and my aunt's name too," I said, but I could tell this Linda was going to be different. "Do you have a family moving here with you?"

"Nope. It's just me." We tugged together on the stakes, but nothing budged. I saw the sweat beading up on her golden brows, little specks of humanness. I loved her already.

"I don't want to alarm you," I said, "but most of the people in Fauntlee Hills are pretty elderly. My grandma June lives next door, and she's eighty. She's also about as private as she can be, given that she's an original resident, but most of these folks are epic busybodies."

At this Linda laughed out loud. "So, are you a busybody too?"

"Me? Oh, most definitely. But I'm also a kid, one of the only ones around. I'm happy to offer my weeding services for a negotiable rate. All local gossip is free of charge."

Linda pushed her glasses back toward her eyes and studied me a moment longer. "I'll keep that in mind."

She was eager to go inside, so we left the pickets with their swinging hooks until Linda could unpack her tools. When I looked back and saw her carrying a fine brown briefcase—not unlike the one my father took to work—I shouted, "Hey, Linda! Are you a career woman?"

She laughed again. "Well, I'm twenty-nine years old, I have a full-time job, and I pay all the bills. I guess that makes me a career woman."

After that, I waved to her from the lush green lawn, turned a couple cartwheels, tried to play it cool. In my journal I wrote in my giddiest script: *I guess that makes her Mary Richards!*

(Loose-Leaf Insert)

DRAMATIS PERSONAE

TED B: Anchorman at WJM-TV and the only member of
the news team not fired by the new station manager on
the final episode. In some ways, his character rivals
Mary's for most changed over the course of seven years,
and in terms of life circumstances, his definitely
change the most. When the show begins, Ted is a vain,
insecure, and largely incompetent single man who has a
tendency to alienate men and women alike. By the end
of the series, he has found true love with Georgette,
become a husband and a father, and learned how to be a
better friend to the people he once took for granted.
He even turns down an impressive job in New York City
to stay at WJM. In one of my favorite episodes, Ted
has a heart attack and (temporarily) becomes much
more generous and compassionate. At the time of this
writing, he is the only deceased member of the MTM
cast, a fact I cannot believe, let alone accept.

GEORGETTE F (LATER B): She makes the "opposites
attract" saying seem true, since her character falls
in love with Ted despite all his bad habits and his
difficulty committing to their relationship long-term.
Where Ted has too much ego, Georgette has too little,
so maybe they balance each other out in the end. Rhoda
and Mary worry that Georgette is living her life as a
doormat for men and women alike, so they try to help
her assert herself more. There's a scene where she and
Ted both wear tuxedos to the Teddy Awards, which is
thrilling to me because I've always thought it would
be fun to wear a tuxedo and Georgette wears it so well.
She says, without any sense of malice or judgment, "I
think we look like the top of a gay wedding cake." That
was interesting to note.

(15)

(Loose-Leaf Insert)

LOU G: Lou Grant, who Mary always calls Mr. Grant, is the producer of the Six o' Clock News at WJM, and when Mary becomes Producer, he becomes Executive Producer. Even though Lou has three grown daughters, he's not the kind of person you want for a father so much as the kind of person you want for a mentor. His daughters make appearances on the show occasionally, and you get the sense that he never tells them the truth, or at least that he is never completely honest with them, the way he is with Mary. He coddles them more than anything, but with Mary, he practices a "tough love" that proves much more beneficial in the long run, I think. His wife Edie leaves him early on in the series, then marries someone else. In the second-to-last episode, Lou goes on a date with Mary, which ends with laughter rather than romance. They have the most chemistry of any two people on the show, so it's nice to learn that chemistry doesn't have to be "sexual."

BESS L: Daughter of Phyllis, who actually calls her mother "Phyllis." This would not fly in my house, I can tell you that. Mary, in her role as "Aunt Mary," often ends up playing go-between for Phyllis and Bess, and in a really edgy scene—probably groundbreaking for the time—gives Bess her first sex talk. Another time, Bess is rebelling against her mother and basically moves into Mary's apartment. Later Bess shows up looking like a hip teenager, going out on dates, etc. The actress who plays her retired from show business and just lives a normal life now, or as normal a life as is possible for a former child star.

PHYLLIS L: Phyllis isn't a very sympathetic or likable character on the surface, and yet you find yourself feeling for her, especially when she learns her husband Lars is having an affair with Sue Ann, a

colleague of Mary's at WJM. It's ironic because Sue
Ann isn't very sympathetic or likable on the surface
either, so maybe the real question is why Lars is
drawn to these kinds of women? He never appears on the
show in person, but Phyllis often imitates his Swedish
accent when recounting something he said. When this
happens, you lose track of whether you're laughing at
the content of the statement itself or at how Phyllis
has presented it, and probably, at least some of the
time, you're laughing at both. The show is full of lots
of complex layering like this.

RHODA M: Rhoda is vivacious and witty and creative
but tends to date "feebs"—her word for losers. She
diets a lot in the early episodes and then seems to
reach her goal weight around Episode #54, where she
wins a beauty pageant at work. She's originally from
the Bronx, and she introduces Mary to the difference
between "Midwestern love" and "Bronx love," which she
explains comes with a fair amount of guilt. She lives
in the attic apartment at 119 North Weatherly, which
is decked out in wild shades of pink and orange with
a clothing rack instead of a closet, and instead of a
giant R on her wall, she has a gold "etc" that I love.
(Mary has a closet, but Rhoda doesn't, which I think
is a comment on the fact that Mary keeps some things
private, even from her viewers, while Rhoda always,
literally, wears her heart on her wide bell sleeves.)

SUE ANN N: Sue Ann is a home economics guru who
hosts a cooking show called "The Happy Homemaker,"
filmed at WJM-TV. While she is "man-hungry," first
carrying on with Lars and later seducing Lou with
plenty of other men in between, she's also the only
female character on the show who owns her own home,
and you get the sense that she has reached a level of

financial success where she no longer has to worry too much about her day-to-day expenses. This may be another version of making it on her own and one notable reason to admire Sue Ann's savvy in a "man's world."

MARY R: Mary Richards is our protagonist, of course, the character we are primed to identify and empathize with throughout the show. The show's creators chose to keep her real-life first name as her character's name. This means she is the only person on set who is called "Mary" when cameras are rolling and when they're not. (I do wonder if this creates any identity confusion for her, though, since she is forever linked by a name with her most famous role.) There are a lot of differences between the two Marys. Mary Richards is single for the duration of the show and has never even been married before. Mary Tyler Moore has already been married and divorced once before the show begins and has remarried Grant Tinker, one of the show's producers, to whom she stays married for the show's duration. Mary Richards doesn't have children, but Mary Tyler Moore has a son who is a teenager during the Mary Richards years. You can see that she keeps a picture of her real-life son on the set, though—on that little table by the window. The character Mary Richards eats meat and drinks moderately and says early on that she has never smoked because she was afraid it would stunt her growth. The actress Mary Tyler Moore has Type I diabetes and is both a vegetarian and a recovering alcoholic, meaning no meat and no alcohol in her life at all. She also used to smoke three packs of Chesterfields a day, which is a startling fact I learned from her biography. And though Mary Richards is genial and moderate in her attitudes and beliefs, I find it notable that such an overtly feminine character has the initials "MR." See? Slyly subversive after all!

MURRAY S: Murray is a news writer for WJM whose desk is positioned next to Mary's. He and Mary are close in terms of proximity within the office and close in terms of worldview and—as we learn in a later episode—also close in IQ. They remain friends throughout the show, and near the end of the series, Murray confesses that he is in love with her. This puts Mary in an awkward spot, but she handles it with her signature (and oxymoronic!) graceful nervousness. In terms of names, which are always important markers of character, it's notable that "Murray" sounds so much like "Mary," and also that Murray is married to a woman named "Marie," which is another form of "Mary." (I should know since Marie is my middle name!) This triad of similar names suggests that Mary, Murray, and Marie are locked in a strange kind of love triangle. Mary isn't romantically interested in Murray, though Murray is attracted to both Mary and Marie. Marie really likes Mary, but there is always an undertow of anxiety that suggests Marie worries about Murray's feelings for Mary—and of course this makes sense, given Murray's actual infatuation with her! More evidence of the complex layering that makes me love this show.

EVEN A SHADOW KNOWS THE PLEASURE OF BEING CAST

Though I spent much of my youth staring at the television and willing myself inside, I also wanted to act, to feel myself fleet and in motion. So when Linda B. came to live in our neighborhood, I pondered how I might write myself into her story using the only template I had.

On the inaugural episode of *Mary Tyler Moore*, thirty-year-old Mary Richards arrives in Minneapolis and moves into a new apartment. She is the outsider in this script, the woman who comes from elsewhere—single, and for the moment, unemployed. She meets Rhoda, the window-dresser who lives upstairs, and despite a bad first impression, their friendship is foreshadowed from the start.

Phyllis, who lives downstairs and who we later learn actually owns this building with her husband Lars, signs a lease for Mary before she has even seen the place. Talk about names and their appropriation! Maybe this is why Mary carries her golden letter M to every place she lives, hangs it on the wall right at eye-level. I suspect she is trying not to forget who she is and trying equally hard not to be overwritten by others. Maybe, in time, she will collect the rest of her letters.

We learn right away that Phyllis is a difficult person: calculating and headstrong, obsessed with appearances, not to mention unfailingly blind to nuance. She appears in this script as the natural analog to my mother. And Phyllis, like my mother, has a daughter—just one—*Bess*, who teeters always on the brink of disappointing her. I know this brink too well.

So it dawns on me that I will be Bess to Linda B., understudy to her version of adult womanhood. Remember the episode early on where Mary takes Bess on an outing downtown? They get ice cream and play hide-and-seek around the fountain in the square. They laugh and talk and seem to really hear each other. This montage is eventually embedded in the show's second set of opening credits, commemorating the way Mary becomes the Not-a-Mother Bess must have been dreaming of. And Linda, though she bears my mother's name, is adoptable as Not-a-Mother for me, that crucial foil.

"What is it you do exactly at Linda B.'s house?" my father asks one night. We are eating dinner, and the brown Magnavox in the corner is watching us for a change.

"I don't know. We talk, and sometimes I help her in the garden."

"You never help me in the garden," my mother says without looking up.

"Well, she pays me," I recover quickly, "which is good for my college fund. And besides, she hasn't lived here that long. I'm kind of like her local guide or her—*informant*." This is the kind of sleuthy word I like to use.

"I hope that doesn't mean you're telling her anything you shouldn't." Now my mother trains her eyes on mine and won't release them until I nod my compliance. "What I'd like to know," she continues, "is whose truck I see parked in her drive-way till all hours. Sometimes that truck is there for the whole weekend."

The truck in question belongs to Patrick, who has been Linda's boyfriend before and who will be Linda's boyfriend again. Their relationship has an on-off switch. She loves him but still has doubts about their future as a couple. I suspect he is a Dan Whitfield sort and that, in the end, Linda, like Mary before her, will have to break his heart.

"Do you know anything about that truck?" my father asks.

"Um, I think it belongs to a friend of hers. He has to travel sometimes, so he leaves his truck there."

"Well, what woman her age has *friends* who are *men*?" This my mother says as she spears a stubborn green bean. "Isn't she at all concerned about her image?"

Now my palms turn slick, and words stick to the trap door inside my throat. Clearly, my parents haven't watched *Mary Tyler Moore* as closely as they've been watching Linda B. The fact was, Mary stayed over at men's houses. Once, she came back to her apartment in the morning still wearing her evening gown from the night before. The show was saying plenty about sexual freedom without saying anything directly at all.

It seemed obvious to me, though a bit jarring at first, that I needed to be catapulted out of the 1950s of my daily life and into a future era. Mary wasn't married, but Mary had sex. Mary was a Modern Woman. And if Mary was having sex and being modern in the '70s, then Linda B. could certainly have a boyfriend who slept over in the '90s. She even had an adjustable shower head to accommodate the men, past and future, who had stood or might someday stand naked in her tub.

Of course I knew better than to say such things to my parents.

"That truck might actually belong to her cleaning lady, now that I think about it." This was half true. Linda did have a cleaning lady, but Laurie actually drove a sedan.

"A cleaning lady!" Now my mother drops her fork and makes a grand gesture. "Well, la-ti-dah!"

"No, no, Linda isn't like that—not a snob or anything. She just works a lot, you know—sometimes 60 or 70 hours a week. So it helps to have another pair of hands."

"Well, your mother worked that many hours a week before you were born, and she still kept a lovely home for both of us. No outside help required," my father declares.

Sometimes I wonder if my mother is feeding him his lines, a little crib sheet passed beneath the table.

For a few moments, nobody takes a bite. Chewing in such tense silence is inadvisable. Finally, my mother sighs and resumes eating, granting permission for us to do the same. "All I know is that if Linda B. thinks she has it tough now, just imagine the rude awakening coming her way after she has a husband and child of her own."

Did Linda B. even *want* a husband and child? This was a good question. She had stayed friends with her ex-boyfriend, Bruce, and sometimes she cooked dinner for him and the woman he married—Nan. This struck me as the height of classy and enlightened, the way Linda didn't begrudge them their happiness. Maybe she was understudying *them*, rehearsing for her own life as a future wife and mother? And hadn't she mentioned being godmother to a different ex's kids?

There was clearly a lot of investigating to be done, but I kept coming back to the question, *What about Mary?* She talked in the show's first seasons about marriage and motherhood as though they were ultimate destinies. Then those statements gradually tapered off. The reason could have been changing times or different writers, but I wanted to believe the reason was Mary herself—Mary, growing further up; Mary, still evolving.

By the time Dan Whitfield asked her to marry him, she diagnosed his proposal this way: "You're in a mood to get married, Dan, and I'm not." Just the fact that marriage could be part of a mood, which everyone knew was only a shade away from a whim, delighted me—an implicit refutation of my mother's mantra that her life didn't begin until the day she met my father. The corollary was worse: "And I didn't become a woman until I became a mother." I gagged and wrote *Gross!!!!* on the nearest notebook page.

THE MARY/RHODA
REVERSIBLE RAINCOAT

Before long, I brought my friend April to spend time with
Linda too. April was willowy, with a pert nose and a credible
fashion sense, which made her Mary-esque. When we were
together, I always played Rhoda, a part I took to well. I liked
Rhoda's wisecracks and self-deprecation, not to mention her
deep thoughts—like the time she said she wanted to learn
how to sit alone in a room and truly enjoy the company. I
wanted to learn that too. Plus, Rhoda knew how it was to have
a challenging mother. Linda Wade was about 40% Phyllis
Lindstrom and about 60% Ida Morgenstern. And finally, on
a more frivolous note, I was crazy about Rhoda's many colorful
scarves.

I asked my mother if I could borrow some of her things from
the '70s—for a school project, I may have said, or maybe for
Halloween. She had a tie-dyed shirt with a beaded peacock
on the front, a denim purse that had once been the top of a
pair of pants (just imagine!), and in her vanity she directed me
to a drawer dedicated exclusively to kerchiefs. Opening it was
like tugging on a magician's sleeve. Or, as Rhoda once said of
a messy room: "It looks like the inside of a goat's stomach in
here!" *Strong simile*, I noted, and the audience roared. When I
played Rhoda, I could also practice my humor, learn what to do
with a laugh.

In February 1992, April and I prepared a special cake for Linda's thirtieth birthday. The body of the cake was chocolate, and with wobbly pink icing, we wrote, *Welcome to your Mary Richards' years!*

Of course we baked this cake in Linda's kitchen, using all of Linda's ingredients, and then we toasted her with our first taste of real champagne. It came from a bottle called Brut that Linda opened when we asked if she had any Martinelli's sparkling cider.

"Thank you," she smiled, blowing out all thirty candles with a single, self-assured puff. Then as she cut her own cake into admirably sized pieces, Linda pronounced the words that sent April and me spinning: "I hear you say it all the time, but you're going to have to fill me in on who this Mary Richards is."

"Who she *is*?" April sputtered.

"But you were even alive for first-run viewing!" I gaped, rising out of my chair.

Linda sat calmly, poured herself some additional champagne, and continued licking the frosting off the candles. "Can you be more specific? I've been alive for a lot of things."

"Mary Richards—from *The Mary Tyler Moore Show*." April spoke slowly as she began to braid her hair. "Julie got me into it, and now I'm *way* in. Like, *way*. Have you really never seen it before?"

"Oh, sure. I saw it a few times. I just forgot that Mary's name was Richards on the show."

"What did you think of it?" I asked, placing my hand over my heart as if preparing for a flag salute. "Are you a fan?"

Linda shrugged. "Fine, I guess. I mean, it was the '70s, and I was busy being a kid and then a teenager. I wasn't thinking too much about who I wanted to be when I grew up."

Incredulous, April and I exclaimed in unison: "Mary Richards!"

"I get it. That's her name."

"No—*Linda*, you grew up to be Mary Richards! *You are* Mary Richards to us!"

At this, Linda laughed and stood to rinse her hands. "But isn't Mary kind of a goody-goody? Couldn't I be Elaine from *Seinfeld* instead?"

I wasn't allowed to watch that show because my mother said it promoted loose morals and birth control for unmarried women. Though when you thought about it, *if* you did: Mary must have been using birth control too. Otherwise, how did she date so often and never find herself "in a motherly way"?

"She's not a goody-goody really," April replied. "And as the show goes on, she gains a lot of confidence. She learns how to take a stand for what she believes in. She blossoms into her best self."

Linda dried her hands with a dish towel and rejoined us at the breakfast nook. "So—the Mary Richards' years? What does that mean?"

I raised my hand as if to say, *I've got this.* It was, after all, my phrase. "OK, so the show ran from 1970 to 1977, and Mary is thirty when it starts and thirty-seven when it ends. So now you're thirty, see, which means you're just starting your Mary Richards' years—better put, your *Mary years*—a time of unprecedented personal growth and self-discovery!"

"Well, I'll take your word for it," Linda replied. Her mouth was serious, but I could still see the smile in her gray-green eyes. "Here's another question, though: do you really have to wait until you're thirty to begin such an important quest?"

"Oh, we're training for it now," April assured her, fork aloft. "But it helps, you know—to be looking forward, to have Mary out there on the horizon. She's kind of like our lighthouse so we don't crash into the rocks."

NEW CELLULAR WOMEN

Linda never fully embraced her title as our honorary Mary Richards, but she did give April and me an exceptional preview of coming attractions—and in some cases, revulsions—of adult womanhood. We learned more from her than from our own mothers and cable television combined. Linda's mother had died when she was in first grade, and we speculated privately that this fact may have accelerated her coming of age as a wise and confident woman. *Could the Mary years be different for everyone?* we wondered. *And was seven years important, even symbolically?*

"You know how they say in science that it takes seven years for your body to completely regenerate its cells?"

April was painting her toenails, but she seemed to be listening. "Uh-huh."

"Well, if you think about it, that means we're new cellular women every seven years. It's a fresh start from the inside out. So the Mary we meet in the pilot episode and the Mary we send off during the series finale doesn't just *seem* different—she actually *is!*"

April reached for the Acetone. "*That*, my friend, is a very deep thought."

"And it's true," I beamed, "because of science!"

SEASON Highlights

LINDA ON TAMPONS:

"There is nothing to be afraid of. And if you are afraid, you can wait to wear them until you start having sex. But the most important thing is not to wait until you start having sex to get to know your body. You should be the first person to pioneer that territory."

MARY ON TAMPONS:
[Crickets]

LINDA ON DOUCHING:

"There is no reason a woman should be made to feel that she has to douche. I've done it before, but that was a personal choice, and I probably wouldn't do it again. This culture, as it stands, is completely obsessed with controlling women's bodies, particularly how we smell. You don't need any powders or perfumes or scented lotions, and you definitely don't need to buy anything that targets your intimate areas. No 'feminine deodorant sprays' and no douches. Any man who really loves you is going to want to bond with your scent."

MARY ON DOUCHING:
[More crickets]

LINDA ON FEMALE DESIRE:

"Every woman is different. Don't let anyone tell you that there's only one thing you can like or want or feel. I have a friend, and she doesn't like kissing on the mouth. It just isn't her thing. It doesn't turn her on. But it took her *years* to admit this to herself, let alone to anyone she was dating, because she thought people would think she was abnormal. Frankly, some people did. But you aren't living your life for other people, are you? And if you can't be honest about what you want, it's going to be pretty hard to get it."

MARY ON FEMALE DESIRE:
[Even more crickets]

LINDA ON RELIGION:

"No, I don't own a Bible. No, I never really got into any of that—church or Sunday school or even bedtime prayers. I don't see much point in being an atheist, which requires taking and defending a position on God's *non-existence*. But I don't see much point in being religious either, as it requires taking and defending a position on God's *existence*. So, yeah, if I had to say I'm anything, I guess I'm an agnostic."

MARY ON RELIGION:

During her interview for a secretarial position, which is upgraded to Associate Producer at WJM News, Mary's future boss asks what religion she is. She tells Mr. Grant he isn't allowed to ask that question of a job candidate, and he replies, "Wanna call a cop?" At this, she blushes and shakes her head no. When he switches gears and asks if she's married, she blurts out,

"Presbyterian!" then stammers, "Well, I decided I'd answer your religion question instead."

This is all we ever learn about Mary's religious heritage, but omission is a powerful force at work on the show. That is, viewers never see Mary attend church, and we never hear Mary pray or evangelize anyone. We can merely infer she is a non-practicing Protestant.

In a real-life interview, Mary Tyler Moore explained that she had been raised Catholic but did not consider herself a religious person. I wrote in my journal:

Since Catholics and most Protestants are baptized as infants, is there some kind of "drying procedure" that allows us to reverse the ritual if we choose? *

I left this entry starred, pending a future answer.

LINDA ON LESBIANISM:

"Well, you know, my housekeeper Laurie is a lesbian. [I didn't know!] She has a nice girlfriend named Jane, and they seem really happy together. [She does? They do?] That, to me, is the bottom line. [See also: Linda's commentary on female desire.] If you're doing anything just to make other people happy, or just to prevent other people from being uncomfortable, then you probably want to reconsider. It wouldn't feel right to me to be with a woman, but that isn't because it's wrong for someone else to be. Laurie told me that when she dated men, everything felt wrong to her, like a left-handed person using a pair of right-handed scissors. She wasn't saying that dating men should feel wrong to me, you know, just that it didn't feel right to her. And knowing what you feel shouldn't lead to prescribing those feelings for other people."

MARY ON LESBIANISM:
[Deafening crickets.]

[I don't know yet why it's important to me that Mary Richards is socially progressive, particularly on a topic like this. After all, I want to like boys. I want to be popular and desirable to my future dating pool. Why should I care if Mary Richards would be friends with a lesbian, let alone if she ever felt a more-than-friendship feeling for a girl? I want to like boys, and I insist I like boys, and yet. . . . I find this is a sentence I cannot finish.*]

NEWSWOMANHOOD

"Here's what we know, *definitively*," April summarizes as we lounge on lawn chairs in Linda's backyard. "Mary and Rhoda and even Phyllis, surprise, surprise, are members of the Concerned Democrats of Minneapolis. That's encouraging, you know—values-wise. They're liberals."

And Linda, we knew, was a Democrat too, another startling difference from the Fauntlee Hills status quo. In fact, Linda B. may have been the first Democrat we had ever met in real life. This was exciting to consider but also dangerous to reveal. When my mother found out the pastor's wife had met President Clinton, she refused to shake her hand after worship. "I don't want to catch anything," she said.

If she found out that Linda B. was a Democrat—let alone that her cleaning lady was a lesbian—I might be put to soak in a tedious bath indefinitely, with nothing to read but William Bennett's *Book of Virtues*. Somehow I had already received three copies of the tome, one of which even contained a personalized message.

"And remember when Phyllis thinks her brother is dating Rhoda, and she doesn't like that idea at all, but then we find out that he and Rhoda are just friends because—jaw drop—Ben is actually gay?" I nod. April has made an insightful point. "Mary doesn't say anything much either way, but she definitely doesn't freak about Ben's orientation."

Linda, who is refilling the bird feeder and tending the rhubarb and raspberry plants, intercepts us now at this pause in our conversation. "My turn," she says, with an impish grin.

"Now I get that you both are incredibly loyal fans, and I admire how you put so much time into analyzing every aspect of *The Mary Tyler Moore Show*—almost like it's a subject in school and you're aiming for a 4.0. But why *this* show? It was already off the air before you were born."

"Don't remind me," I sigh. "I missed it by two years."

"I only missed it by one," April says, with a rare glimpse of one-upmanship. "But in the end, a miss is still a miss."

"And a ma'am is still a ma'am!"

We burst out laughing and then between giggles try to explain about the episode where Mary is called "ma'am" instead of "miss" for the first time and takes it as a sign she's getting old.

"But—OK, OK." Linda tugs the brim of her baseball cap, the one she always wears while working in the yard. "I see you're nostalgic for a time in which you didn't live, but why not a show centered on people your own age? I'm just curious. Why not *The Wonder Years*? That show's on now, but it's about kids growing up in the '60s and '70s."

"You know, Bonnie, the school secretary, gave me an autographed picture of Fred Savage," I say. "He wrote *May all your years be wonder years*, which was a nice touch, I thought, but I'm still holding out for an autographed picture of Mary Tyler Moore."

"How many days since you sent her the letter?" April asks.

"Sixty-four. But I understand it takes time to reach a really famous person, and I'm willing to wait."

"That still doesn't answer my question, though," Linda says. "Mary belongs to the 1970s, and she was born—"

"*April, 1939*," April beams. "We don't know the exact date, so we can't be sure if she's an Aries or a Taurus. I'm inclined to say Taurus though, based on typical characteristics of the sign."

"Mary Tyler Moore was born on December 29, 1936," I add, "which means she's a Capricorn, a sign that fits her remarkable determination—"

"Enough!" Linda calls a truce by raising her trowel. "You each receive a valedictorian medal for your knowledge, but let's stay focused here. Mary, the actress *and* the character, is a child of another time. Any way you slice it, she's two generations removed from you. Explain to me the appeal."

We look at each other, and then April starts tugging at some clover, her version of a pass.

"Come to think of it"—I am stalling now—"you *do* look a lot like Winnie Cooper on *The Wonder Years*." April really did: right down to her slender shoulders, long straight hair, and the small pink bow of her lips.

April just rolls her eyes and laughs. "Do not."

Finally, I say: "Linda, no disrespect or anything, but you've got it all wrong. You think people are living in one time or another, but I'm pretty sure I'm living in three. Fauntlee Hills is the '50s, *Mary Tyler Moore* is the '70s, and the rest of the world—*Calendar World* and *Nightly News World*—is the '90s. Maybe Mary is just the best bridge for a really large gap."

April stops tugging at the clover now, and Linda puts down her trowel. "OK," she nods. "That was really—I—OK."

"Sometimes Julie does that," my friend vouches for me. "She says something, and it's really smart, and you want to put a note after it like 'End scene' or 'Curtain falls'."

"And you don't think of your Aunt Linda as Mary Richards because—?"

It is a leading question, but these are my favorite kind. "Well, I love her—like a whole lot—but she's not exactly what I would call a Modern Woman. She has her own apartment and a job in an office building and even a swanky Mustang like the one Mary Richards drives, but those are just surface similarities. She's here, you know, at my grandma's, every weekend. She calls to check in with her mother every night even though she's almost 50 years old." I take a deep breath because I know what I'm about to say is something I shouldn't. "Also, she only wears pads, and she's saving herself for marriage." I tug the clover too. "It all seems like a placeholder to me, *pretend-grown-up*—like she's not really independent at all, just an older girl waiting for a prince to come and hold out a fancy shoe."

"Hmm." Linda is good at listening without judging. She walks back toward the house and begins to unravel the hose. After a while, she says, "Well, I am flattered to be your role model—"

"Oh, we think you're terrific!" April gushes. "We've been talking about how we'd like to make you an honorary board member of our detective agency."

"Definitely! We'll even put your name at the top of the letterhead we're designing for important mystery memos and such."

"Mysteries are good," Linda nods. "Sleuthing is fine. But Mary Richards was a newswoman, right? What about putting all your curiosity to good use and doing some investigative journalism?"

April and I eye each other, then spring to our feet in tandem. We are mouthing the words *investigative journalism*, and it's clear we both like the sound of them, this new heft on our tongues.

"So—would we—we'd just—?"

Linda has the sprinkler going now, and we all stand in the grass admiring its gentle arc and surprising range of motion. "Why not start a newspaper? You like to nose around in other people's business, and you like to write." She tugs her cap again. "If you make it legit, you could charge people something for each issue, sell ongoing subscriptions at a discount, that kind of thing. *And* you'd add something else to your college applications." Another pause. "Parents like that, right?"

"Oh my God! They do! They really do!" I am overheating with excitement now, peeling off my shoes and socks despite the cool weather. "We could report the local news—like *super-local*—missing pets and petty crime in Fauntlee Hills! We could even interview the neighbors about any number of things and let them advertise their garage sales with us at a better rate than *The West Seattle Herald!*"

"I could do a fashion column," April volunteers, "and horoscopes too! I could even make surveys to get a more interactive component going!"

We are jumping up and down, running into the sprinkler fully clothed.

"Let's call it *The Fauntleroy Gazette!*" I shout.

"OK!"

"We'll be the editors-in-chief, and Linda can be our editorial adviser!"

"OK!"

But then April does the Mary thing and turns practical for a moment. "We'll need some office space, though, and some way to actually print the paper."

Linda, halfway up the back stairs, calls over her shoulder: "You can use my computer—once a month." We like the fact that she always sets boundaries with us. "When you're done out there, dry yourselves off, and we'll have a look at some two-columned templates."

We mouth the words *two-columned templates*. They taste good to us, grown-up and accomplished.

"Maybe," I murmur, "we can even figure out a way to leave smudges on all our subscribers' hands!"

w.w.m.d.

Of all the things I ever said I wanted—kissing and more than kissing, whatever that might entail; moving the tassel on my graduation hat from one side to the other and tossing it, Mary Richards style, high into the air; driving my own car into a strange city and signing a lease on a cozy studio apartment with a balcony and a fold-out couch; accepting an offer from the CIA or FBI or a comparable organization committed to worldwide snooping and spying; and of course publishing my first book, which my mother insisted would only be worthwhile if I managed to outsell Danielle Steel—I did not know if any one of these, or even all of these in sum, could transform me more completely into a human hot air balloon rising from the earth in pure elation than receiving an autographed picture from Mary Tyler Moore.

I sent her a fan letter. It was long, detailed—part televisual analysis, part personal testimony. Then I waited. And waited. And waited.

After 98 days, each square on my calendar marked with a squiggle and an optimistic *Not yet*, I returned from school to behold the black-and-white **DO NOT BEND** durable envelope rising like rare obsidian from our mailbox. Before my mother had even finished braking, I stood breathless on the porch, tearing along the seam, then guiding the 8 x 10 glossy from its protective sleeve. It was her—the Mary of the moment, a woman in her middle fifties with a striking short haircut and a turtleneck sweater. She had written with fine-tipped pen,

40

Julie, Many thanks for caring! and below that, her signature, which I recognized from the autographed script—*Mary Tyler Moore.* Authentic, bona fide, inviolable.

Was this how astronauts felt when they blasted off into space? I had defied gravity after all! I had made contact with a woman so marvelous she might as well have been another life form! The return address, I noted, wasn't even California. It was New York City, where I knew from a recent documentary that Mary Tyler Moore lived in a penthouse overlooking Central Park, with her third husband Robert and their dogs, Dudley and Dash. I had reached her. I had finally reached her!

I let my school bags drop to the ground. I let my mother holler about homework and chores and not being late for dinner. With the envelope tight in my hand like a relay baton, I ran full tilt toward my grandmother's house, she who had gently cautioned against "getting my hopes up." *Celebrities don't always have time to answer letters from teenage girls.* I would show her—not in a gloating way, but in a joyous, I-always-knew-she-would-come-through-for-me way.

But as I crested the hill, I saw Linda's house, and I recalled how she had said she would take me shopping for my eighth-grade graduation (shades of Bess and Mary, no less!), let me pick out something I liked all for myself over which my mother had no control. And though it was only a little after four on that late spring afternoon, I noticed her car parked at the curb, wheels turned just so—her car like an invitation.

I didn't stop to think how she was picking up her new beau at the airport; how she had told me this fact only yesterday to prevent me from stopping by unannounced or leaving rambling messages on her phone machine that echoed throughout the house. But in my altered state, I forgot all these things and flew instead through the front door, calling out "Hiya!" the way

Rhoda often did, followed by a "You'll never believe this, not in a million years!" And then there was Linda sitting close to Simon on the couch, white wine in the glasses beside them, and a *holy shit* gleam in their eyes.

These were not the first adults to dispel silent profanities in my presence, but still I could not refrain:

"Linda! Linda! It's here! Mary Tyler Moore sent me an autographed picture, and now I know what I want for graduation—a really beautiful, elegant, perfect frame!"

"So then what happened?" April wants to know. Ten minutes later I'm sprawled on my grandmother's bed, Mary's likeness propped on her pillow, the phone pressed close to my ear.

"Well, it was pretty awkward. For all I know, they could have been making out just seconds before I arrived. But once I realized what was going on, I apologized, of course."

"And did you leave—I mean, pronto?"

"I left, but I showed them the picture first." April sighs. "Well, how could I not? It's the whole reason I barged in on them in the first place!"

"I'm not sure an apology's going to cut it. Linda might be mad at us for a while."

"Not at *you*. Why would anyone ever be mad at *you*?"

"Oh, we're a package deal, and everybody knows it." For some reason, this makes me smile.

"Should I write her a letter?"

"Linda?"

"Yeah, you know—try to explain what the picture means to me and how it may have clouded my judgment—"

"Just let this blow over, OK, Julie? You already apologized for ruining her date and generally acting like a psycho." April laughs a little, to lighten the mood. "I think the thing to do in these kinds of situations is to ask yourself, *What Would Mary Do?*"

"*Not* write the letter and go next door and put it in Linda B.'s mailbox?" I wince as I say this out loud, remembering the episode where Mary tries to dissuade Rhoda from sending a how-do-you-feel-about-me letter to a man she has just started dating. Of course Rhoda still sends the letter, and of course it's a huge mistake.

"Bingo." April is slurping her Cup o' Noodles now, but I know she means what she says. "If you think it will help, I can make you a bracelet: *W. W. M. D.*"

I think it would help a lot.

AUGUST AND EVERYTHING AFTER: A PROLEPSIS EPISODE

Linda B. did forgive me, which was a Mary Richards kind of thing to do, and she also reassured me that it wasn't my fault when she and Simon broke up a few weeks later. They just weren't compatible. For my part, I practiced writing

W. W. M. D.

over and over in freshman calligraphy class, establishing my expertise with these four capital letters above all the others. When Sister Janice asked what they stood for, I told her, but I got the distinct impression she thought I meant the Virgin Mary.

Speaking of Virgin Marys:

LIKE ME, MARY TYLER MOORE

. . . attended an all-girls Catholic high school. Hers
was called Immaculate Heart, and mine was called Holy
Names.

[Both intrigued me conceptually.]

Sometimes I tried to picture what it meant to have
an immaculate heart—like a little dollhouse in your
chest, all the feelings neatly tucked and stowed? My
mother was fond of saying: a place for everything

[love, fear, hope, rage? . . .]

—and everything in its place. Or was an immaculate
heart more like a tidy carport? Surely no power tools
cluttering the three spare walls.

[Only room for one shiny wagon or pure intention at a
time; no competing impulses or contradictory desires.]

And what about a holy name? No name was more sacred
to me than Mary, be it Mary Richards or Mary Tyler
Moore.

[I even secularized the "Ave Maria" in my head
as we sang the homage during weekly Mass.]

In one interview I read, Mary described herself as
a "good girl" who lost her virginity on her wedding
night. She noted that she was only eighteen at the time,
a new high-school graduate eager to strike out on her
own.

[Yet it didn't escape my notice that she chose a husband—ten
years her senior, no less—to help her complete the leap.]

Within a year, that Virgin Mary became Mother Mary to
an unplanned baby boy.

[Contraception and abortion, I inferred, were equally
unthinkable in that 1950s as in mine.]

They named the child Richard after his father, almost
as if Mary had nothing to do with him. The whole Jesus
story—[I noted precociously in an early "featured editorial"
like this]—went down in an eerily similar way.

Over the next four years, April and I wrote, typed, printed, and sold 50 issues of the *Fauntleroy Gazette*. We charged 50 cents per issue, with a discounted rate of $5.00 per year at Linda's suggestion. In any given month, we had 25-30 subscribing households, and we hand-delivered each issue as part of our personal-touch philosophy. The final edition featured a Clip Art banner of mortar boards, with the tassel moving progressively from right to left:

It's time for us to move on!!!

we announced in Monotype Corsiva, and the issue included a retrospective of our favorite stories.

Of course many of the biggest stories of those four years were intimate and emotional, not journalistic. They happened out-side the scope of our public reportage.

For instance, I started running a lot. My father used to ask what I was running away from. I thought myself clever when I told him I was running toward. "OK—toward what then?" he asked. And that was where I faltered.

The future seemed a copout thing to say, given that it was coming anyway. But was there something I could do to hasten its arrival or to alter its shape? I didn't know. I was jittery, and I couldn't say why. Running helped to soothe me, to steady my nerves. And I learned that if I joined the cross-country team at Holy Names, I'd have the opportunity to letter.

To letter. I chewed these words hard and kept them close at all times, perpetual as a cud. Before the coach said so, I never knew *lettering* was a process, that *letter* could ever be a verb. Maybe this was how Mary Richards earned her golden M? She had been a cheerleader in high school after all, a fact I skirted, tried never to dwell on too long. I feared it meant that she and I could not have been friends in the immaculate Roseburg High of my imagination.

So I ran for the team. At first, I was just good enough, and then I was better than average, and then I was promoted to Varsity, which was another way of saying that I had lettered.

"What do you think about when you run all that time?" April asked. She didn't go to my school, and running wasn't her thing. Like Mary, she favored ballet. She knew how to exercise pretty, how to stretch her muscles out long instead of bunching them tight. "It's just so far, and I know that if I didn't pass out, I'd be hopelessly, miserably bored."

I told April the truth: that I thought a lot about television and also about films. I replayed favorite scenes in my mind, and if there were songs, I always sang along in my head. Music helped to set the rhythm of my footfalls. I liked theme songs best, and the *Mary Tyler Moore* theme song, written and performed by Sonny Curtis, was especially strong. I loved how both versions began with questions, but the first season's question was credible: "How will you make it on your own?" The episodes would reveal the answer. After that, the question became rhetorical: "Who can turn the world on with her smile?" Duh. Mary can! And just like that, she appeared—Mary, divine in her winter coat, haloed with sunlight, smiling.

I told April the truth, but I didn't tell her everything. Omission was a powerful force at work in my story too. I thought about women. I thought about Elizabeth Montgomery as Samantha Stephens on *Bewitched* and Barbara Feldon as Agent 99 on *Get Smart*. I also thought, relentless as a spinning record, about Jodie Foster as Clarice Starling in *Silence of the Lambs*, a movie I wasn't supposed to have seen.

But when I thought about these women, I didn't want to be with them like a good friend at dinner parties or on stakeouts or running the obstacle course at Langley. And I didn't want to *be* them either, doing all those things by myself. It was a different feeling, perhaps one without a name, which was ironic since Agent 99 didn't have a name either. She only had a number. This feeling I had seemed nameless, and the days of keeping it to myself felt numbered too. It would all add up, I feared, to something undeniable.

My parents permitted me to watch a few contemporary TV shows, like *Dr. Quinn: Medicine Woman* and *Touched by an Angel*. Similar nameless feelings arose when I saw Jane Seymour hike up her pioneer dresses to avoid the mud or Roma Downey toss her auburn hair that seemed to perfectly match the color of Della Reese's convertible. The jitters came from looking and later recalling their bodies on the screen—from something low in my belly that wasn't hunger exactly but wasn't not-hunger either. I wanted to touch them, I knew that much, and every time I recognized this longing, I pulled my mind back like a hand from a hot stove, a camera panning out to a more aerial view.

And then I thought about Mary. She was my salve for the thing that was burning.

Such relief to realize I didn't want to touch her; that I didn't feel the hungry not-hunger in my gut when I watched Mary or Rhoda or Phyllis; that I didn't feel it in later seasons when I watched Sue Ann or Georgette either. I didn't feel it even when Georgette performed her dance routine to "Steam Heat" at the Teddy Awards, her body unquestionably lithe, her top hat and faux tuxedo beguiling. I scanned my body: no deep ache, no covert quiver. I was free when I thought of them, rounding the final turn on the three-mile course, sprinting toward the finish. They were women I loved and admired, laughed with and even laughed *at* sometimes, but they were women I did not ever, even once, desire.

During this time, April's parents began sleeping in separate rooms. Her father had fallen in love, he said, with another woman, and he took April and her sister to meet this woman and her kids. There was talk of divorce for a while, and then there was no talk at all, and I knew April was living in her own kind of limbo, a namelessness she would not discuss.

We didn't know why love stopped or changed. We didn't even know why love began. But April developed a two-pronged strategy for coping with all the uncertainty in her life: collect tiaras and find a boyfriend.

She had always liked sparkly things, and some part of her must have also wanted to become one. Some part of me wanted to be April, wanted to like sparkly things and the thought of turning into human glitter for Prom. But somehow I didn't believe there were enough sequins in the world—or enough neck kisses from boys who drove Volkswagen bugs, for that matter—to putty the gap between who I was and who I was expected to be. Instead, I spent a lot of time saying, "I like this one, but that one's nice, too," and learning second-hand about second base.

When Coach Boyle called me to his office to claim my letter at the end of the year, I ran. What else was I going to do? I burst through the door and held out my hand, awaiting the J that would align my life visibly with Mary's. Sure, it would be smaller than Mary's M, which had been enhanced for television, and yes, I knew it would be fabric instead of copper, but that didn't mean I couldn't hang it on a wall or tack it to my bulletin board. Maybe I would even want to wear it on a jacket someday, to keep that J with me all the time.

"Congratulations," he smiled, and into my palm he placed a gray felt H with dark maroon trim—our school colors.

"There must be some mistake," I replied. "Is this Hannah's letter?"

"Oh, no," Mr. Boyle smiled again, scratching his midday stubble. "They're all Hs. The letter stands for Holy Names."

In my journal, the entry simply reads: *WHAT THE H?*

Also during this time, Linda got serious with a pilot named Paul. Shortly before we graduated from high school, they told us that Paul would be moving into the Fauntlee Hills house. "It's big changes, all around, for everyone," they smiled.

April and I wanted to be happy for them, we really did, but it was hard. We were eighteen and seventeen, respectively, which meant we found it easier to be self-absorbed, to believe that we should change while everyone else remained the same. We were the parade after all, and we needed others to stay in their place on the sidelines. How else were they going to cheer for us as we passed gloriously by?

Thank God for re-runs, I wrote. *They are the only things we can count on these days, the only safely foregone conclusions.*

A flashback episode

When I was thirteen, stuck between the end of *middle* and the beginning of *high*, Linda drove me to Southcenter Mall for a special outing. She bought me lunch at a bistro with hot bread and cloth napkins, then took me inside a fancy shop to pick out a picture frame. I still don't know why she did it. Maybe she thought she'd never have kids of her own? Or maybe it's easier to be kind to a kid someone else bears the burden of raising? (They're likely to appreciate it more.) I doubt Linda even saw much of herself in me, though we did share a certain ambition—she the mother-less and I the over-mothered—some deep-seated need to "make it on our own."

I chose a sterling silver frame with a black velvet stand. The frame could be hung from a wall or placed upright on a desk. Silver would go well with the black and white of the photograph, I thought, and Linda said I had a good eye for contrasts. We put the picture of Mary Tyler Moore into the frame right away, so it wouldn't get wrinkled or warped. The clerk wrapped the frame in tissue paper, but I kept peeking at it all the way home.

On our drive we listened to The Counting Crows, an alternative band Linda liked a lot. She played them while we worked on our newspaper, and I grew to like them too. It was August, and the album was called *August and Everything After*. This made me think about the impending school year but also about the future at large.

These songs were poignant, I thought, and they conjured a sad, conveyor-belt feeling, a sense of dread about all that was nameless but inevitable ahead.

As she turned from the main road into our neighborhood, and I felt the vault closing behind us—that heavy, invisible wall— Linda asked me something I couldn't answer, something that caught me completely off-guard: "So, what happens after the Mary years are over?"

"To Mary?"

Linda shrugged. "To any of us. Thirty-seven isn't so old, you know. Or maybe you don't know yet, but you will." We had crested the hill. We were coasting more than driving now. "I can see it from here, that thirty-seven," she said, "and it doesn't look like an ending to me."

LAMONTS MIGHT HAVE BEEN MY WJM

THE FIRST INTERVIEW

I wore a purple pant suit and the pumps of a much older woman. On my lapel: an angel holding a small Swarovski crystal ball. This was a gift from Grandma June for high school graduation. "I know how much you like that angel show," she smiled. I wanted to say, *Don't remind me.* I wanted to say, *I don't need Roma Downey and her pretty hands and Irish brogue getting in my way today.*

The store was called Lamonts, and it had been operating in Seattle since 1970, the same year *The Mary Tyler Moore Show* premiered. I considered this fact a most auspicious omen. My parents, who once described their own love story as a "whirlwind retail romance," met at Sears in 1963. My father was a manager-in-training, my mother a college student recently hired as a sales clerk in Shoes. It took more than three years of courtship before they actually tied the knot, so I always raised my eyebrows at the "whirlwind" part.

"Shouldn't I apply to work at Sears?" I asked. "Isn't it a proud family tradition or something?"

"It's *too far* to drive," they replied in unison, which meant they had probably discussed the prospect before. Too far in this case meant seven miles, with no highway traffic or difficult merging—really, just a straight shot up 35th Avenue to the West Seattle Junction.

Lamonts, however, was easily walkable from home, and by car, only a swift five minutes away. Someone could always pick me up or drop me off without too much inconvenience, since I didn't have a car of my own. The store belonged to a little island of commerce called Westwood Village, where we had shopped for everything—clothing, groceries, hardware, stationery, toiletries—for as long as I could remember. I knew Lamonts, and though I was never a fan of shopping, particularly with my mother, I favored the store for nostalgic reasons—the way they had preserved the past so completely they might as well have called it Pompeii.

That is, inside Lamonts, it was *still* 1970. And until the day the doors closed forever following a second bankruptcy, it was always 1970 inside Lamonts.

The original carpets, frayed and stained—worn completely bald in places so bits of floor peeked through—retained their bodacious orange and yellow patterns. The fitting rooms retained their built-in ash trays, and despite the No Smoking signs added to each entrance, some customers had been known to light up out of habit while trying on nightgowns or slacks. Once I found a stubbed-out Pall Mall still smoldering in the Ladies Sportswear fitting room. The lipstick was so fresh that the culprit couldn't have made it farther than the London Fog display.

The restrooms were huge, like mausoleums, with a lounge full of mod couches and garish mirrors that visitors passed through on their way to the stalls. On the counter, I ogled a translucent bowl of potpourri—larger than an eagle's nest—perfuming the room with its deluge of cinnamon and cloves. Oh, yes—and in the jewelry department, an actual disco ball dangled from the ceiling! I imagined the after-hours parties where surely Lamonts hired a DJ and all the employees danced.

But these were regular business hours on a Thursday afternoon, and someone had to page Larry Bodmer three times before the slight, middle-aged man appeared on the selling floor and escorted me into his office. Could he be my Lou Grant? I wondered. His black hair had thinned to greasy threads, and the worst kind of comb-over was in play. *Would he pour himself a cup of coffee, then slyly mix it with liquor from his bottom drawer? Would he be gruff with me but simultaneously tender? Would we have witty repartee culminating in his assessment that I had spunk?*

"Remember," Linda warned, "that doesn't mean the same thing today as it did then."

Mr. Bodmer looked, to say the least, bedraggled. He grunted as he reviewed my résumé, then set his glasses down on the desk and rubbed his bloodshot eyes. "So how long, reasonably, do you think you'll stay?"

"Well, I'd like to work full time in the summers and over holidays, and I can even work part-time on busy weekends during the academic year. I'm going to college in the fall, but I won't be very far away."

"College." He nodded. "That's good. Where?"

"Pacific Lutheran University," I said softly.

This was the school where my grandfather had sent my father his junior year as punishment for "having too much fun" at the University of Washington. There were no frat houses at PLU, no athletic teams to speak of, and at the time, no dances or social clubs. It was a school where students were expected to concentrate on their studies and where free time was filled with chapel and choir. I was most embarrassed about the "Lutheran" part.

But somehow, at this disclosure, Mr. Bodmer brightened. "Terrific! Are you interested in the seminary at all?"

"The seminary?"

"I'm a deacon myself," he said, "but I'd like to work as a minister full-time. Granted, I've been saying that for the last 20 years, but one day, God willing, I'm getting out of here."

"So—you wouldn't say that retail is your calling?"

At this, he snorted. "*No*. I would say that retail is my cross to bear."

I noticed, with some chagrin, that there were no pictures of Larry Bodmer as a young football star lining his stark paneled walls. There was no old-fashioned coffee pot quietly perking or classic brown mug made in a daughter's pottery class. Just a nametag, a notepad, and a Jesus fish used as a paperweight.

So maybe he wasn't Lou Grant exactly, but that didn't mean I couldn't be Mary Richards.

"I'll do a really good job," I promised. "Both my parents worked in retail—that's how they met—and my dad went on to manage several Sears stores after that."

"Hmm." Larry folded his hands on the desk, then cracked his knuckles one by one. "It doesn't look like you have much work experience, though I am intrigued by this little newspaper you ran."

As if taking cues from a stage hand, I slid toward him the final issue of *The Fauntleroy Gazette*. "Just in case you'd like to see it," I smiled. He put his glasses back on, wet his thumb, and flipped through.

"Horoscopes, huh? That's a little witchy."

"Oh, my friend wrote those. They're not meant to be taken too seriously. And we don't mess with Ouija boards or anything."

"Well, look, I'm not gonna sugar-coat this," he said, and I perked up at the gruffness such a statement seemed to portend. "We get a lot of nuts in here, shop-lifting is on the rise, and I can only offer you minimum wage. But if that sounds like what you're looking for—put away a little money for school, get some experience working a register, interacting with the public—then you'll be fine. Maybe your next job can even be halfway decent."

"So what you're saying is, *If you don't like me, you'll fire me! And if I don't like you, you'll fire me!*" I grinned, hoping he would recognize the reference.

But instead, Mr. Bodmer's forehead creased, and he rubbed his eyes again. Finally, he said, "Well, if you don't like me, just keep it to yourself. Everyone else does. And if I don't like you, it won't be a problem—unless you show up late or start stealing from the till."

"Oh, I was just quoting from—never mind." I stood up and stuck out my hand. I strained my dimples to offer my widest smile. "Thank you, Mr. Bodmer! I will gladly accept this position! And I promise you won't regret hiring me!"

He squinted as he stood, touched my hand lightly, replied, "You can just call me Larry. We're not that formal around here."

NEARby

Remember when Mary Richards signs up to be a Big Sister? I think this was the first time I realized—in a tangential thought—that she, like me, was actually an only child. *How had it taken so long to connect these salient dots?*

Lou suggests Mary will struggle mentoring a delinquent youth because she's too wholesome, too sheltered, the same vexing insinuations people always made about me—vexing, most of all, because they were true.

Mary defends herself by saying: "I've been around, Mr. Grant... OK, well, maybe not *around*, but I've been *nearby*."

I had been nearby too—literally. I had been two-miles-on-foot and five-minutes-by-car from the Westwood Lamonts all my life. I knew the layout, I knew the merchandise, I knew the hours they were open; I even had the store phone number memorized for times my mother made me call to see if they had such-and-such in a certain size or style. Why should I worry about not being worldly enough to make small talk with customers or fold a thin layer of tissue paper around their purchases before slipping them into a bag? Why should I worry about being too sheltered to change the receipt tape on the registers or clean out the fitting rooms? I had a pant suit after all, and my AARP pumps, and enough pairs of thick brown pantyhose to take up bank-robbing in my spare time.

But of course it wasn't the work that made me quiver a little in my low scuffed heels. It was the other employees, most of them women, most of them older—with their Nicorette gum and their Prado handbags and their *I've-seen-a-thing-or-two-so-nothing-could-shock-me-now* faces. These women had exes and stepkids and grandkids, unpaid parking tickets, restraining orders, sponsors, rhinestone-studded nails. Creditors sometimes called them at work. Angry lovers sometimes loitered in the parking lot, screaming their names. They were women who knew how to change a tire and chug a beer. They were also women who knew how to get someone to change that tire for them and pick up their bar tab at the end of a long night.

I loved them at once, you see. I loved their humor, which I didn't always understand, the stories they told about bachelorette parties and blowjobs, which I had to look up. Mortgages and miscarriages unsettled me more, but I loved them for their bravery and their cunning and their sheer will to survive.

It was strange to realize I didn't need to be a sleuth at a job like this. No conversations were covert, so no investigations were required. These women shared everything, spilling their guts over Lean Cuisines in the breakroom and Marlboro Reds just outside the back door. By the end of my probation period, I had become a playwright. I liked to think I was living the play, but in truth, I watched most of the crucial action from the wings. Sometimes I consoled myself with a mantra: *Mary was nearby, and so am I.*

DRAMATIS PERSONAE

CINDY B: Never wanted kids; raises parakeets with her husband, Carl; they have matching leather jackets, even though they don't look at all like the kind of people who would wear leather jackets; they also drive matching Mazda Miatas in parakeet yellow and blue; no idea whether their families support their interracial marriage or not.

CYNTHIA B: Loves her husband very much; doesn't drive and relies on him for rides to work as well as a lot of emotional support; two of her siblings have died tragically (this was true of Mary Tyler Moore, too, who lost her sister at 21 to suicide and her brother at 47 to cancer, becoming an only child herself by her early 50s), and after many miscarriages, she gave up trying to have children. She was also mauled by a dog as a child and is paralyzed with fear whenever service dogs come into our store.

ELAINE G: Immigrated to the U.S. from Scotland after a bad marriage; has three grown children in the States and mostly babysits for her grandchildren when she isn't working at Lamonts; can't afford to divorce her husband, who still wants her back but is abusive. What if she falls in love with someone else? Does this mean she can never marry again?

ROBIN J: Bears a strong resemblance to Morgan Fairchild from Mork and Mindy, and other women at work seem to think she's vain. She works in the main office, not on the selling floor, and she lives in Fauntlee Hills. I once trick-or-treated at her house. Robin has two little boys, but the man I thought was her father

or maybe even her grandfather is actually her husband!
I checked with my grandmother, and apparently he's
lived in the neighborhood a really long time. Now he is
old and retired, and my parents refer to Robin as his
"trophy wife."

LINDSAY K: Sells shoes for the store and lives with
her boyfriend, who is sometimes volatile and lashes
out. When she has to leave him for a while, she goes to
stay with her mother, Nancy, who also works at Lamonts
and still has a lot of younger kids at home. Lindsay
showed me these sticks in her arm that are supposed to
keep her from getting pregnant for five years. I forget
the name, but she called them "implants" of some kind.
You're not supposed to smoke when you have them in, so
she's trying really hard to quit.

NANCY K: Lindsay's mom, who smokes several packs
a day and has been married five times; two of her
previous husbands are in jail, but that doesn't seem
to scare her; she says she's most afraid of driving,
so she takes the bus or has Lindsay take her wherever
she goes. Her smoker's cough is scary, but her laugh is
hearty and real.

KAREN M: Has been at Lamonts for over 20 years;
always wears a three-piece dress suit with heels that
are many inches high. She is kind, never crude, but
also believes in very old-school things, like tall
bangs shellacked with hair spray (think of the kind of
wave that surfers seek, and you can picture her hair),
heavy foundation that conceals all her pores, and a
full corset. Her husband must help her with the laces;
that's all I can figure.

(Loose-Leaf Insert)

SHIRLEY: Used to work for Sears but doesn't remember my parents—I asked. Married twice, divorced once, widowed after, heavy smoker, and one of my favorite people in the world. Lonely, I think, even though she seems to drink and play cards with a group of friends on a regular basis.

DEBBIE W: Just found out her husband has been cheating on her for years and now that their kids are grown wants to marry his mistress. This news came at the same time she received a diagnosis of early-stage multiple sclerosis. Debbie is, understandably, furious with the world. A lot of her conversations revolve around male strip shows and seeking revenge.

TAMMY W: Currently involved with a guy named Craig; thinks he could be "the one." She loves all things Disney and wants to go on a Disney cruise. If Craig wants to marry her, that's probably where he should propose.

LINDA Y: Her teenage daughter is recovering from leukemia. Ordinarily, Linda doesn't believe in tattoos, but her daughter wanted to get a tattoo at the site of her surgery scar, so Linda took her, and they got tattoos together. I can see how it would be nice to have this Linda as my mother.

SEASON HighLighTS

EXIT STRATEGY:

My official Lamonts placement is in Ladies Sportswear, working with Cindy and Tammy. If they're short-handed in Lingerie, I might be sent over to help Shirley or Linda. More occasionally, I'll give breaks to Debbie and Elaine in Jewelry, Cynthia in Children's, or Karen in Men's.

My official Lamonts nametag includes my title: *Sales Associate*. I'm pleased to note the way this phrase echoes Mary's *Associate Producer*.

"Now before we get started," Tammy says, sizing me up from her dotage behind the register, "I have a few questions for you."

I nod with vigor. I'm holding a tiny Steno pad on which to take my training-day notes. My pencil is where all work-place-themed television has led me to believe it should be: tucked behind my ear.

"Be nice," Cindy murmurs, and when she catches my eye, she says, "I meant Tammy. You're probably always nice."

"So, how old are you?" Tammy has long thin hair my mother would call dishwater blond, and she is fond of pulling it back in a variety of Disney-themed scrunchies. Today's features Nala from *The Lion King*.

"Seventeen," I say, then make the essential allusion—"No hedging, no *how old do I look?*"

"Well, if I were judging by your face, I'd say you look about twelve, but if I were going by your clothes, I'd say sixty-five." I'm not sure how to respond to this assessment, and Tammy laughs so hard I can see the back wires of the grown-up braces she wears.

"What did I tell you about being nice?" Cindy sighs.

"Oh, I'm just having some fun with her," Tammy says. "Rule number one: *Do not get trapped here.* What's your exit strategy?"

"I'll probably just leave through the front door—unless there's a separate door for sales associates?"

"Wow. OK." Tammy looks at Cindy as if to say, *Is this chick for real?* I have seen this look before but cannot always predict when it will surface.

Cindy is busy pinning sensor tags to a batch of sweaters on a roll-out cart. Her glasses are small and round, and if I had known who John Lennon was at that moment in time, she would have reminded me of him.

"Tammy's right about this one: you've got to have an exit strategy. Otherwise, ten years will go by, and you'll still be working here."

"Well, I start college in the fall, and—"

"Got it! Everything's starting to make a lot more sense now. You're a college girl. And let me guess—you were a cheerleader in high school." Tammy mimes pom-poms and the obligatory *rah-rah-rah.*

At this, I gape, not sure whether to be offended or flattered. After all, if Tammy could mistake me for a cheerleader on my first day, she must have glimpsed something in my manner or appearance that was reminiscent of Mary Richards.

"Well, don't just stand there, Cheer Girl." Tammy motions for me to step behind the counter, familiarize myself with the rows of bags and boxes, applications for store credit and thirty-day Layaway. "I'm going to make this really easy for you. You'll ring everybody up, and I'll sit here on this nice little chair and watch. No better way to learn than trial and error."

Cindy wears a polo shirt tucked in with a pair of pleated slacks. This is her standard costume. The colors are always drab, which makes the magenta she applies to her lips that much more surprising. She rolls her eyes at Tammy, then turns to me. "In between customers, you'll almost always have freight to tag. We try to get it out on the floor as soon as we can."

"Tammy," I ask, looking over my shoulder, "what's the second rule?"

"Huh?" She is biting her nails, a magazine already spread across her lap like a napkin.

"You said before that rule number one is not getting trapped. What's rule number two?"

Tammy looks at Cindy again. "Do you believe this kid?" Her round face and red cheeks glow. "Write this down in your little notebook. Rule #2: *Don't get trapped*. Rule #3: *Don't get trapped*. Rule #4: I think you get the picture."

OUR LADY VICARIOUS:

Most of the full-timers work the day shift, which means they leave at 5 PM. I work from noon to close, covering their lunches and handling the evening rush. Some part-timers come in each night from 5-9, and one of these is a new hire named Lisa.

Like me, Lisa has recently graduated from a local Catholic high school, though hers was co-ed. She is college-bound in the fall with her boyfriend Matt to the University of Washington. Already they are planning to get married in a few years, which proves a kind of skeleton key, an easy way to unlock doors of conversation with the older, more experienced women.

This is how things work in Lamonts World: If you have a man in your life, you're automatically enfolded in the discourse. If you've just been jilted, or if you're carrying a hopeless torch, you've got enough material for some kind of speaking part. Recall that Mary Richards had a broken engagement to a medical student named Bill. That fact alone would carry her across the threshold, even though her would-be groom never did. But me? I didn't have much in the way of romantic history. Most of my life had been lived through pages and screens, and my favorite mood, as Sister Mary Annette once declared with notable derision, was "the subjunctive." In a furious journal entry, I even canonized myself `Our Lady Vicarious, looking on as everything happens to everyone else.`

So it occurs to me that maybe I should be jealous of Lisa, that I should covet her future coming so clearly into view while mine remains foggy as windshield glass on a winter morning. One of the first things she asks: "Do you have a boyfriend?"

I shake my head. I'm embarrassed, likely blushing, but I can't say I'm too sad about the actual absence, only about what a boyfriend could do for my clout in the breakroom.

"Don't feel bad," Lisa smiles. "I mean, Holy Names is an all-girls school. It's not like you've had much of an opportunity."

"Right. I mean, what was I supposed to do—take a girl to Prom?" We both laugh awkwardly, and then I have the urge to scrape silt from my tongue. *Oh, the bad taste this leaves in my mouth!*

TRANSITIVE PROPERTIES:

Lisa and I work a lot of nights together—weekends too—and we both stay on with Lamonts even after college begins. She confides in me about her struggles with weight, how lucky she is to have a guy who doesn't mind. I come to realize that Lisa regards me in much the same way Rhoda regards Mary, which is not unlike the way I regard April.

For the first time, the transitive property from math class makes sense in a real-life way. To be female is to be always watching, always keeping tabs. How was I any better than the old people in my neighborhood? In any given room at any given time, I knew who was smaller than I was and who I was smaller than. We were sizing each other up, even and especially our friends. We were making assessments about each other's normalcy and attractiveness, and—as a consequence—who was most likely to find (and be worthy) of love.

It sickened me, but I couldn't stop.

There's an episode of *Mary Tyler Moore* called "Put on a Happy Face" where Mary is struggling palpably—everything going wrong in her life at once. She doesn't have a significant other at the time, and Rhoda's steady boyfriend Jonas is taking her on a trip to Mexico. Here's what Rhoda says about their lives:

"You're having a lousy streak. I happen to be having a terrific streak. Soon the world will be back to normal. Tomorrow you'll meet a crowned head of Europe and marry. I will have a fat attack, eat three hundred peanut butter cups, and die."

I could imagine Lisa saying something similar to me. We didn't grow up together after all. She didn't know much about where I came from, or the restrictions with which I was raised, let alone my elaborate fantasy life. She simply assumed, because I was taller and thinner, I must have been fated for greater happiness.

And though I didn't think it was true, I was willing to indulge Lisa's perception of me. This was my chance to *be* Mary Richards, to move into the driver's seat of her stylish life and take command of the wheel. How strange to be seen as someone normal and attractive, someone destined for a traditional happy ending.

Lisa was good at persuading customers to apply for the store credit card. I watched her in action and memorized her script. For each applicant, whether or not they were approved, the soliciting employee received $2.50 in Lamonts bucks. These we could use as cash for shopping in the store, and coupled with our 25% employee discount, items on the clearance rack often ended up costing us nothing at all.

For the first time in my life, without my mother's foreknowledge or consent, I began purchasing my own clothes. The older women had a habit of saying, "I wish I could wear something like that!" and then they looked over at me. Everything was relative. Here, in this place, I had the mannequin body. I could model fashion and manifest sex appeal. Admittedly, all the styling was out of my hands, but the attention fit like a pair of fine red Isotoner gloves. I didn't care if I liked the clothes; I cared that everyone else did. Soon my colleagues were picking things out for me, setting promising outfits aside as soon as they came in or once they were marked down: shirts that slipped off the shoulder intentionally, a skirt with a slit up the side, dresses of all kinds.

"You look like a million Lamonts bucks," Tammy grinned at me one day. "Now go clean out those fittings rooms so I don't have to!"

I liked her candor. I also liked watching myself sashay down the mirrored hallway, confident in my sleek black slacks and the mauve boat-neck blouse that accentuated my long neck and collarbones.

As was our way, I called back to her: "It's like the inside of a goat's stomach in here!"

"You're weird, Cheer Girl," came her chuckling reply. "You're weird, but I like it!"

TOO GOOD TO BE TRUE:

By sophomore year of college, I was living a double life. School Me was nerdy, clumsy, and quiet. She didn't know how to do the late-teen thing in the late 1990s, let alone how to prepare for a whole new century that was also a new millennium. Talk about the pressures of reinvention!

School Me dated guys but had crushes on girls. She went through a bad hat phase but never owned a Mary Richards tam. As with elementary and secondary school, she had the distinct impression that nobody she met in university life ever really understood her jokes. And despite the popularity of the show, she always disdained *Ally McBeal* as an ersatz version of *Mary Tyler Moore*. And *Murphy Brown?* Forget about it!

Lamonts Me, on the other hand, could hear "Love is All Around" swelling in the background every time she strode through the double doors and clipped her nametag into place. She smiled at everyone, and everyone smiled at her. She was good at her job, and she knew it. She was good, too, at making other people feel good about themselves. Too bad her position didn't come with commission.

When Tim, the regional sales manager, was closing out with her one night, he said, "You could have a real future in retail, you know that? You're management material if I've ever seen it."

She thanked him and relayed the obligatory story about her father and his Sears stores.

"Don't take this the wrong way," Tim said, lifting the blue money bags out of her hands, "but there's something different about you. You seem a little—too good to be true."

He might have said: "You seem like you come from a fictional town." She would have believed him.

NINETEEN TO THE NINES

For my nineteenth birthday, I wanted to go out with April dressed to the nines. Nineteen, as she knew, was a special number in MTM cosmology. The first episode aired on September 19, 1970, the final episode aired on March 19, 1977, and for the first five years of the series, Mary lived at 1-19 North Weatherly. To commemorate this occasion, we would appear in character—both of us playing unique versions of Glamorous Mary on Teddy Awards night.

The women at Lamonts had already selected two Wonderbras for me—white lace and black lace—plus pink lace panties that read *Naughty* and *Nice*. They used phrases like "If you've got it, flaunt it," and "You're only young once." Despite my blushing, I bought whatever they chose.

But one day as I was sifting through fitting room discards, I came across a long black dress. It had spaghetti straps and a faint shimmer of gold in the fabric, a subtle iridescence. I remembered a photograph I had found in a library book, which I promptly photocopied and pasted into one of my scrapbooks. It was a 1960s publicity still of Mary Tyler Moore as Laura Petrie, years before she transformed again into Mary Richards. In this photograph, she stood tall, like she was holding a pencil between her shoulder blades. She was an actress after all and had been trained how to pose. The dress accentuated the hourglass shape of her body. Never fond of jewelry myself, I loved that the dress was everything—she wore no necklace, bracelet, or earrings. There was only a hint of cleavage and then her long tapered form.

When I tried on the dress, I had never resembled MTM more: my stiff hair, my bright eyes, my large mouth. And was it only my imagination, or had Mary also seemed a bit aloof in that photograph? I would have to check, but I thought I remembered the way she stood with the man (Dick Van Dyke) but apart from him too. I sensed a small thread of apprehension woven through her, perhaps a hint of a question—*Am I pulling this off? Will the audience believe me?*

A green clearance tag indicated that this dress had been marked down: from $120 to $100, then half of that, then half of that again. I bought it the second my break began.

"What's in there?" my mother asked, pointing to the garment bag on the back of my door.

"Oh, a little birthday present for myself," I smiled.

"Well, let's see it," she said, her arms crossed, her body blocking the threshold.

Things had been delicate between us. My mother liked that I was taking an interest in my appearance for once, even though she frequently reminded me that I had missed my chance to excel at pageants. *Where was this feminine, fashion-plate daughter when I needed her?*

I took my dress into the bathroom to change, which my mother didn't like. She found my modesty in her presence suspect, proof I must be hiding something. But when I opened the door and stood before her, more Mary-esque than I had ever been, I felt certain she would praise me, that the pulsing in her temples would slow. Imagine my surprise:

"*No.*" And her finger was even wagging when she said it, which some critics would call over-acting. "That is *way way too sexy* for a nineteen-year-old girl to wear."

"What?" I looked down. "I'm hardly showing any skin at all."

"It's hugging your body all over the place. It's calling too much attention to your curves." She wagged her finger again. "*Absolutely not.*"

"But Mom!"

"But nothing. Take it off. You'll return it at work tomorrow."

"April is waiting for me! I have to be at her place in 20 minutes!"

"So she's waiting. So what? I have something else you can wear."

The replacement dress was a heavy fabric—black body with a square peach jacket, shoulder pads of course, and gaudy gemstone buttons. The dress didn't move with me so much as in spite of me: flattening and boxing me, limiting my stride. I looked like a missing child snapshot on the side of a carton of milk. Estimates for how old that child would be today placed her age somewhere close to forty-five, fifty maybe.

When April opened the door, she said only, "I'm not going to ask." I thanked her, and then I cried.

WHAT WOULD MARY DO?

Once my fifth-grade teacher came into the store. By this time Tammy was pregnant with her first child, and Craig was making routine chimichanga deliveries on the hour. I waited on everyone and took care of the fitting rooms, too, feeling useful as an understudy promoted on opening night.

"How may I help you today?" I said, but this time when I looked up, Mrs. Kolbe was standing there. She had seemed a giant before—a gaunt witch on stilts—but now I was fully grown, and to my surprise, we met each other eye to eye.

She glanced at my nametag, to be sure, and then she said, her lip curling—but not in a friendly way: "Why, Julie Wade! I don't believe it."

"In the flesh," I smiled, but my heart was tapping its fierce Morse code: *What would Mary do? What would Mary do?* Mary was all that held me steady in that moment, kept me from raising my middle finger, from denouncing her in front of everyone and then walking swiftly away.

"Did you find everything you were looking for today?" I asked.

She nodded and handed me a few garments—Rafaela blouse, Liz Claiborne ankle-length slacks, some crew socks presumably for her husband.

"How funny to run into you here!" Tammy sipped a Big Gulp in the background, and Cindy sorted jeans by size into the plastic cubby holes nearby. "Likewise," I replied. *What would Mary do?*

"Have you been working at Lamonts long?" Mrs. Kolbe's face still reminded me of a scrub brush, and when she stared at me, I could feel the bristles passing over my skin. *Abrasive* was the word that came to mind.

"About three years now." Our transaction was nearly complete. I kept my shoulders back, my head high. I wouldn't be cowed, but I wouldn't be cruel either.

"You know," she said, but her saying was more like a scoff as she lifted the white plastic bag with its purple logo, "it always amused me the way your mother said you were going to be a doctor, the way you said you were going to be a big-time detective and best-selling author. Do you remember that?"

I nodded, and I knew Tammy and Cindy were listening now, wondering exactly where Mrs. Kolbe was headed with this line of questioning. "And yet, here you are—selling clothes in a place like this."

It was all I could do not to say it—what I wanted desperately to say: that I was going to college; that I was a junior at a private

76

school on a presidential scholarship; that I was a double major primed to graduate on time and *magna cum laude* no less. But I didn't. I knew what Mary Richards would do, and I resisted a response that could only have belittled the women around me, the women I looked up to, loved.

"Well, you're buying your clothes here," I replied. "If we don't meet your standards, you might want to try Fashion Bug around the corner."

Mrs. Kolbe flashed me a menacing smile, her little fang-teeth showing as she sauntered away. Then Cindy came over and stood beside me, slung her arm over my shoulder. After a few moments of silence, Tammy called out from her chair, "Who was that uppity bitch anyway?" We all burst out laughing.

THE HiRiNG / fiRiNG REVERSible RAiNCOAT

In late spring 2000, on the cusp of the summer before my senior year, I call Lamonts to ask about my schedule. Larry Bodmer has left retail for seminary, and a series of other managers have come and gone. Robin in the office is cryptic, puts me on a long hold, and finally a voice I don't recognize snaps "What is it?" into the phone. Don't ask me how, but I can tell instantly that his hair-tips are crusty with gel.

"Hello, this is Julie Wade. I was calling about my summer schedule."

"Who?"

"Julie. I work in Ladies Sportswear."

"For Gottschalks?"

"Excuse me?" He's chewing something, probably gum, so I think I have misheard him.

"For Gottschalks? Are you part of the Gottschalks sales team?"

"Um, I've been working for Lamonts for three years. I have limited hours during the school year, but—"

"Lamonts is bankrupt. Please tell me you know this happened."

"Well, there was something in the early '90s—"

"No, this is the second time. Chapter 11, *the sequel*. They're not coming back from this one."

"But I was just there on spring break, working."

"Times change, sweetheart. What do you want me to say? Lamonts is caput, and Gottschalks bought them out."

"Well, what about—"

"What about what? Spit it out."

I might have said the same about his gum. "Are former Lamonts employees—"

"Some of them are, yeah. We went by seniority. And I don't see you on my list, Janie."

"*It's Julie*," I correct him. "*Julie Marie Wade*." To say my full name feels powerful, like casting a spell.

He pauses, shuffles some papers. "Naw. You're not here, Julie. Sorry to break it to you, but you've been cut loose. I hear The Keg is hiring, though. Lots of people drinking these days, need somebody to serve up those drinks."

"But—" A click, a dial tone. And just like that, a decade before my Mary years have even begun, I find myself out of a job.

THE SECONd iNTERViEW

DIRECTOR'S NOTE: Of course what makes both
Marys so inspiring is their resilience. MTM
was let go from her first job as a dancing
elf for Hotpoint appliances when her pregnancy
became too difficult to conceal. Later she
auditioned but was turned down for the role of
Danny Thomas' daughter on his TV show because
Thomas was convinced that no one would believe
someone with such a small pert nose could be
a member of his family. MR was once fired from
her job at WJM for writing comical obituaries
with Rhoda, one of which Ted ended up reading
on the air. Another time she quits her job
over a divisive argument with Mr. Grant.
(Spoiler alert: He hires her back.) Still
another time, Mary and Mr. Grant go on strike
together in order to secure mutual raises. And
of course, the series ends with her permanent
dismissal from WJM, an event without a known
resolution.

In my own best attempt at being resilient, I make many copies
of my résumé and distribute them to the Human Resources
department of every clothing store in the Tacoma Mall. This
is the closest shopping center to my college, conveniently locat-
ed on a major bus route. It is also my first foray into the job
application process at national chains, which in turn includes
an eerie glimpse of corporate America in action.

Sears never calls. The Bon Marche never calls. Nordstrom's, the fanciest of all the stores, somewhat predictably never calls. But I've already identified myself with Mary Richards, a person who works doggedly for the underdog. And while Lamonts was more underdog than most stores, I'm determined to carve out a niche for myself in the larger retail landscape.

That's when JCPenney calls.

They want me to come in and take an aptitude test, interacting with a computer before I ever interact with a person. I can't imagine yet that this is the wave of the future, a portent from some more-anonymous, less-people-centered world. All of my significant screens so far have been televisions, and I don't realize, let alone believe, that computers will soon make televisions nearly obsolete.

"You're awfully dressed up," notes the woman at the front desk. The way she says it emphasizes the word *awful*, which makes me immediately self-conscious. "They did tell you you're not actually meeting with a manager today, right?"

I nod and follow her down the hallway to a row of computers separated by short cubicle walls. When I take the GRE in a few months' time, the testing stations will resemble nothing more than this corridor with its shadowy figures bent over keyboards under a wan yellow light.

"You can leave when you're done, and we'll call you if we're interested," she informs me curtly.

The test is unremarkable, and I finish in under twenty minutes. Two weeks later I'm summoned to the same dim hallway and told to wait for someone named Caren who will escort me to the conference room.

"Julie! Kylie! Michael!" a female voice barks. When I look up, I see a tall, middle-aged woman draped in waterfalls of gray velour holding a clipboard. "This way!" she motions, and the other twenty-somethings perched on nearby chairs also rise to their feet. I had never heard of a group interview before, but the vibe is that of a distinctly somber game show. Instead of competing for prizes, it seems we might be competing to avoid punishment or even to escape a painful death.

The conference room lacks any markers of a zeitgeist. It isn't the '70s at JCPenney's, but it isn't the twenty-first century either. In fact, as I will later recount to April, we have entered a Room Outside of Time: blue corporate carpet, white regulation walls, and a table that might have been nabbed from the visiting area at a state penitentiary.

"So you're all here because we think you have what it takes to excel as a JCPenney's employee." Caren eyes us over the top of her gold-gilt bifocals. "Currently the department with openings is Shoes. We know you haven't sold shoes before, but that isn't the point. We can train you to sell shoes, and if you decide to accept this position, you'll go to Shoe School for a full week before we put you out on the selling floor."

I raise my hand, and Caren squints at me over her glasses. "You, in the middle—"

"Hi, I'm Julie."

"And—"

"Well, I was just wondering when you say 'if we decide to accept this position' if that means we're all going to be hired for a job today?"

"Isn't that what the person on the phone told you?"

I shake my head. "No. She just said something about a *call-back*."

"All right." Somehow even the freckles on Caren's cheekbones look annoyed. "Well, this is a call-back, and we *called back* because we want to hire you. Everybody clear?"

We nod in unison.

"Everybody here still in the market for a job?"

We nod again.

"Good. Because I'm the manager of the Shoe department, and I don't have time to waste on anyone who isn't committed to joining our team. We're one of the biggest and busiest departments in this store, and everyone works on commission. If you learn the merchandise and you listen to the customers, you can earn a lot of money. If you slack off, your paycheck will reflect that. In the end, slackers aren't really hurting me; they're hurting themselves. And money, we've found, is the greatest motivator for employees to get out on the floor and move some product."

"And then what happened?" April asks. I can hear her loading the dishwasher in the background.

"Well, it was really weird. It was like we were all there in person, but it couldn't have been less personal. Caren didn't call us by our names after the initial round-up, and mostly all we did was sit at that prison table and fill out paperwork. Then she rolled in a television on a cart—this thing was a real anachronism, let me tell you—and we watched a video about how not to sexually harass our co-workers or customers and what to do if they sexually harass us. She didn't even stay until the end of the video."

"How bizarre!" April is going to school part-time at the community college, living at home, and not working. To my knowledge, she has never applied for a job, but much like the matter of her parents' strained cohabitation, this isn't something we discuss. "So how did you know when it was over?"

"I walked out to the main desk with the other applicants, and they gave me a nametag, but get this—it just says *JCPenney*, not my actual name. So all the nametags are interchangeable, making all the employees interchangeable in a way too."

"I bet they want it back when you leave so they don't have to pay to make more for future employees."

April is right, but when I leave this job for graduate school in a year's time, I keep my nameless nametag for posterity and let the company deduct ten dollars from my final paycheck. Some things, contrary to Caren's belief, are not about the money.

THE COUCH MAKES THE WOMAN

One morning I see my roommate's boyfriend and a friend of his pushing a long brown couch out to the curb. "What are you doing?" I call across the courtyard that separates our dorms.

"It's a hide-a-bed," Nathan says. "Just too heavy to cart around anymore."

"Wait!" My eyes are still thick with sleep, but my ears perk at the prospect. "Are you saying there's a *bed* in there? Are you saying that's a *fold-out* couch?"

They both stand upright and stare at me now. "Yeah. So?"

"Well, do you guys think you might like to push that couch just a little bit further?" I make prayer hands to show how serious I am, how grateful I will be. "I know someone who can give it a really good home."

Greg looks at Nathan as if to say, *Is this chick for real?*

"It's old and scratchy," Nathan warns. "My parents had it in their basement the whole time I was growing up. It's from the '70s." He says this like it's a bad thing. "All our overnight guests slept on this couch when I was a kid, but the fabric is so prickly you have to put down a blanket or a beach towel if you just want to sit and watch TV."

"That's OK!" I am grinning and clapping my prayer hands now.

85

"You know, I have a bicycle with no wheels in my room," Greg says, "and the handlebars are all mangled, and the seat's coming apart. Do you want that too?"

"Ha ha! Very funny."

"It's no trouble. I can just run over and get it for you—"

"I have the couch now," I smile. "I might just make it after all."

fit

JCPenney is not my WJM. I know this going in, and I give myself routine pep talks that a true career woman must accept some work as purely transitional, purely for profit. In point of fact, or in point of credible make-believe, Mary Richards must have worked at jobs that weren't especially meaningful for her either, but given the constraints of the script, we never see them.

My mother calls often and never fails to remind me that she was working her way through school selling shoes for Sears at the time she met my father. She noticed him because he met her general criteria of "tall, dark, and handsome," but she pursued him because, in her words, he was "going places." When she tells me "history has a way of repeating itself," I read between her lines and understand she means something more specific: "Keep your eyes open for a man whose name is worth taking."

Caren assigns me to shadow various shoe department employees. The best sales associate—meaning the person who consistently earns the highest commissions—is on vacation, but when he returns, she'll have me spend a day walking in Charlie's footsteps. I giggle as she says it, then foolishly try to explain why I'm giggling. "Well, it's punny, see—" but Caren walks away while I am still speaking.

When Charlie strides into the shoe department, I notice his significant height, his dark features, and his general non-re-pulsiveness. I also notice his beard, which connotes something earthy and liberal that my parents would disparage, and his leather jacket, which seems out of place with the navy suit, but I appreciate juxtapositions more than most people.

When I learn Charlie is 30, I can't help but think of young Mary Moore and Richard Meeker, of their ten-year age gap and their marriage that didn't last. Later I will look back on my notes from MTM's 1979 interview with Barbara Walters—of special significance to me because it was taped the year I was born.

In it, Mary reflected on herself as a young woman: "I really wanted to be independent, I didn't want to be told what to do, and here was this young man to whom I was obviously very attractive and I think I fell in love as much as you can fall in love at that age."

The phrasing always struck me there: "to whom I was obviously very attractive." She doesn't say "to whom I was obviously very *attracted.*" It's more about what he feels for her than what she feels for him—the way his affections become the rope tow for their future romance. Older Mary can articulate the difference in a way that Younger Mary can't.

One day Charlie and I are ringing up a customer, and I can't figure out how to fit the Nine West heels she has selected back in their original box. "You're a writer, right?" he asks. "Think of it this way: the first shoe goes in like a comma"—he nestles it in the crinkly paper—"the second like an apostrophe." Now they fit perfectly.

"But how did you know I'm a writer?" I ask after the customer has signed her receipt and strolled away.

Charlie grins at me: "Well, aren't you?"

SILENT MOVIE EPISODE

The fold-out couch makes everything possible, turns simile into metaphor, me into Mary, more and again. I have not learned myself well enough yet. I have not told myself all of my many truths. At this moment, my greatest female desire is to be legitimized by a man's desire for me. Linda B. would not approve. Mary Richards would not approve. But to be fair, they haven't been in my position, have they? Maybe the same body-pose but not the heart contorted this way, the mind confused. Sex becomes a way to burrow, a time to mute the voice—pretend what I want to like is what I really like. Mary likes men, and for the moment, I am Mary, so this couch-bed is my magic carpet ride. My boyfriend says he loves me; later, that he wants to marry me. But I don't have to say anything when I let myself be taken, taken away from myself into the televisual blue yonder. I think of Mary the whole time, of the post-hypnotic suggestion that accompanies that maiden chime. Mary was going places. Each time he comes, I leave a little less of myself behind. I wander deeper into the script. What scenes can I replay? But always, in the off-screen, these questions are lurking: *What am I running away from? What in the world am I running toward?*

A REUNION EPISODE

At the tail end of the twentieth century, when Linda B. is thirty-seven and April and I are older than we have ever been—*both legal!*, we keep toasting with cheap drugstore wine—we decide a reunion with our mentor is in order. I have gone away to school and stayed away more the past year than I once thought possible. I have a steady boyfriend and a steady job. Yet more than with either of these, I am enamored of the feeling of accomplishment.

Linda agrees to meet for lunch, a lunch we have emphasized by email will be "on us." I want her to know she can have as many glasses of Riesling as she likes, and she can also choose the restaurant where we stage our catching up. The place she picks is called Pegasus Pizza on Alki Beach. When April and I arrive, me having struggled at some length to park my father's car in the narrow parallel spot, Linda is already there, drinking Pellegrino and leaning back in her chair, looking just like herself but—were we wrong to notice?—*larger.*

"This is like the season where Mary gains 12 pounds," April whispers. "She still looks great, but it's so noticeable on her small frame that I guess they felt they had to write it into the script."

"Look at you both!" Linda waves. "Do you feel as grown-up as you look?"

"Sometimes," I say.

"Same here," April echoes.

I'm feeling bashful all of a sudden, even though it's Linda, the woman who has helped me imagine myself into this life— twenty-one, a college senior, applications for graduate school already underway. *Why don't I throw my arms around her neck and effuse my gratitude?*

"Would you like a glass of wine?" I offer, and this a bit more urgently than I had planned.

"No, that's all right," she declines. April nudges my foot under the table. "But you two should have some wine, if you want. I know you've just had a big birthday, Julie."

"Well, you did, too—I mean, like eight months ago, but still. You're thirty-seven!"

April nudges me again, but I'm not sure how to read her signal.

"Ah," Linda nods. "I wondered if you were still navigating by that compass."

"Mary will always be my true north," I reply. The waiter comes, and April asks for a wine list.

"Are you sure you don't want to share a bottle with us?"

"Well, girls," Linda says, then corrects herself—"*women*, either you're too nice to say anything, or you're not as observant as a couple of sleuths should be. But the fact is, there have been some changes in my life of late, and right now I'm not drinking at all."

"Oh my God! Did you get addicted?" I exclaim. This is my younger self, the Queen of Blurt Town, reemerging from the shadows and seizing hold of the conversation.

"No," Linda laughs, and her eyes crinkle at the edges. I notice she isn't wearing her glasses. "A little while ago, Paul and I tied the knot at a small ceremony with his family in Georgia—"

"You got married!" April exclaims.

"Is he in AA? Are you staying sober to support him?" Blurt Town will not behave.

"No, no, nothing like that. I'm staying sober right now because—" she waits, expecting the interruption, but I don't see it coming—"well, because I'm pregnant."

A beat, maybe two, before Blurt Town strikes again. *"On purpose?"* April steps on my foot, hard this time, but Linda only laughs.

"Yes. *On purpose.* Note the haute couture maternity tunic," she says, and winks at April.

Speaking of pregnant on purpose:

A few months before this lunch, I had watched a made-for-TV movie called *Mary and Rhoda*—how could I not?—in which the two friends were reunited more than twenty years after the series' end. I recorded the film but was so upset by the narrative that I erased the tape and never spoke about it with anyone but April again—though I was already trying to write about it:

THE APOCRYPHAL TALE

. . . asserts that Mary Richards married a con-
gressman named Steve and had a daughter named
Rose. When the film begins, recently widowed
Mary arrives in New York—her daughter is by now
a college student at NYU—and ends up returning
to work in television news. No other cast members from the original series appear or are even
referenced during the film, and Mary and Rhoda
seem primarily defined by their roles as former
wives and forever mothers.

"It's all backwards!" I cried. "We're approach-
ing the new millennium, and the only thing they
could think to tell us about Mary is that she
married and had a kid. How unimaginative is
that! How reductive! How—1950s!"

"At least her daughter's an English major,"
April offered.

"So I'm supposed to identify with her daughter
now—her made-up daughter—just because we're the
same age and we both like literature?"

"Well, technically, they're all made up,"
April said calmly. But before I could continue
my tirade, she added, "I didn't like the movie
either, OK? It seemed really forced to me. That
said, I don't think it's wrong for a woman to get
married and have a child or for those things to
be happy milestones in her life. I mean, I want
to get married and have children someday. Don't
you?"

This was a hard question for some reason.
I knew what you were supposed to say, but I
didn't feel like saying it. And I knew what you
weren't supposed to say too, but I didn't want
to hurt April's feelings by saying it. Instead,

I changed the subject, at least partway: "She didn't actually take his name, did she?"

"It said Mary Richards-Cronin in the credits," April replied, beginning to laugh. "Hyphenated is something, right?"

"Something, I guess, but what? CRONIN?" And then we laughed again, the good belly laugh of lasting friendship, and I put Mary back where she belonged—the way, after a long game of chess, the pieces are returned to their origin-places on the board.

When the wine comes, we clink our glasses of Zinfandel with Linda's green bottle and say "Congratulations."

"Have you thought at all about names?" April asks. She seems genuinely happy for Linda—the way I *want* to be, the way I hope at least to seem.

"Well, we like the name Ellen for a girl. Boy names are harder to agree on. Maybe Paul? Maybe not Paul? Maybe we won't ever have to cross that bridge," Linda says with a sly smile.

"What about *your* name?" I venture after a while.

"You think I should name her Linda?"

"Well, Lucille Ball did that whole mother-name-pass-down thing, though I can't say I'm in favor. It's hard enough becoming your own person *without* wearing someone else's name, don't you think? It must feel like that weighted apron they put over you at the dentist right before they take the X-rays."

Linda signals to the waiter for another Pellegrino. "You always did have strong analogies. I hope those are coming in handy in college?"

I nod and blush again. I have the feeling sometimes that she sees me too clearly. "What I meant before—about the name: I know it's none of my business, but I was just wondering—*did you keep yours?*"

April rolls her eyes, but at least she doesn't kick me under the table.

"Yes, I did."

"So just Linda B.—not hyphenated or anything?"

She shakes her head. "Just Linda B., just like I've always been."

Later as we're leaving the restaurant I hug Linda and promise to keep in better touch. It's a promise I'm bound to break, but I don't know that yet, so I speak to her in good faith.

"I'm going to make something for the baby," April says. She takes a lot of craft classes at community college, and I have no doubt she's as good as her word.

"Oh, and Linda"—Her car door is already open, but she turns around, one hand resting lightly on her blue linen belly.

"I'm ready for the post-script," she smiles. "In fact, I'd be disappointed if you didn't have one."

"Well, I just wanted to say—I watched *Seinfeld*. At school, you know. I watched it a lot."

"Yeah? And what did you think?"

"It's really good. *Elaine is fabulous.*"

"I told you. And—?"

"What makes you think there's more?"

"Just spit it out," Linda laughs.

"Well, now that you mention it, I did notice that Elaine's relationships with Jerry, George, and Kramer are similar in a lot of ways to Mary's relationships with Murray, Lou, and Ted."

"Uh-huh." Linda is still laughing as she settles into the front seat. "Some things never change—and sometimes that's a good thing." She waves as she pulls the car door closed, but she also doesn't roll down her window.

"I mean it about Elaine, though!" I shout. "She's a terrific character and also a strong female lead!"

Of course what I don't tell Linda or April or anyone is that Julia Louis-Dreyfus has now joined Elizabeth, Barbara, Jodie, Jane, and Roma inside that secret vestibule where my body abandons my brain.

PITTSBURGH WAS MY MINNEAPOLIS

silent movie episode, with subtitles

The first time I slept with a woman, we were not on my fold-out couch. Her bed was real. Her bed was the thing itself, the thing it was made for, not reversible into anything else. *No take-backs*. Maybe this was the moment I stopped pretending and became my part. For the first time, I was going somewhere without Mary, without the gold coin of possible she had pressed into my palm. *Make a wish*. I did. I was going impossible now. But the Kaufman kids turned that wishing well into a flower pot, didn't they? And Linda B. made everything come up roses like the song. Perhaps a body could be repurposed like a story, rewritten halfway through. Those scissors I had been holding in the wrong hand for years—I didn't need them to cut away the overgrowth. I heard my name in my lover's mouth, and it sounded true: *Julie*. No squinting in the afterglow, only clear sight. I heard my lover's name in my mouth, and it sounded right: *Angie*. Was this an invocation, a celebration, both? Was this me, blossoming into my best self after all?

THE MAIN SETTING

Let's remember that when Mary shows up in Minneapolis, she's a stranger to us. Soon, we'll learn she's had a steady boyfriend for the last two years. We'll discover Bill let Mary "nearly support him" throughout his residency. We'll come to understand they were planning to get married until Bill, testing the perks and prestige of his fresh M.D., posed the question, "Why rush into things?"

But where were they living, and what kind of work was Mary doing, and how did they meet in the first place and when, and who did Mary love before Bill, and if he was her First Great Love, who was her first not-so-great love? In other words, after cheerleading for Roseburg High and the white strapless formal she wore to Prom with the date who turned out to be allergic to her corsage, what happened to Mary Richards? Who was she in the snowy-deep antecedent of Now?

Let's remember that when my beloved and I arrive in Pittsburgh, we're strangers to the place and to the people too. We don't have so much as a Phyllis for close to a thousand miles. *Sign a lease for us?* The prospect, in retrospect, sounds grand. We could be women from anywhere, seeking anything. We're writers after all. We could spin quite a yarn.

But some stories would suit the fringes of Penn's Woods better than others—campfire stories, something to toast a marshmallow to. These people are going to keep asking, "Are you sisters?" "Are you cousins?" "Are you very best friends?" These people are going to keep asking, "Where do you come from, and why do you come here, and why are you traveling together?"

And where were we living and what kind of work were we doing, and how did we meet in the first place and when, and who did we love before each other, and were we each other's First Great Loves? What happened to us before the Keystone, before the long tunnel through the mountain and the three rivers and the delta? What happened to us before the glassy sky like a snow globe and the city with all the bridges inside?

We open the cover and read aloud the first line of the dedication page. Soon they are shaking their heads; soon they have stoppered their ears.

It's true there was a man I might have married, but I didn't. It's true there was a dress I might have worn to my wedding, but I didn't. There was even a ring I took to the pawn shop at the eleventh hour, hawked for small potatoes so my new love and I go could for Thai food and have the sushi too. There was a phone call with my parents that didn't end well, another dial tone reverberating in my ears. *Can you be fired from a family?* There was a ceremony where we could have walked together in our newest caps and gowns, but we didn't. Instead, a hotel, and in the hotel a bed, and in the bed a world we were remaking in our image. No, we never wanted to get up. No, we never wanted to part those curtains and face that world.

Let's recall the lyrics from the first season song: *How will you make it on your own? Girl, this time you're all alone.* There were two of us in the Ford Taurus wagon we called Stella, but we were wondering the same thing as we drove into that twilit city, roads slick with summer rain. *How would we make it on our own?* This was my first car and Angie's fifth. We bought it from a shady auto dealer in Oak Harbor. He rushed the sale, and we signed our names because it had a big trunk and seats that could fold down. "We're moving across the country," we said.

These were the days when *bravery* and *bravado* sounded the same. We signed our names because we were late for a poetry reading and had to get back. This was the kind of trip you can only take once, the ultimate *carpe diem tabula rasa amor vincit omnia*. We signed our names because we didn't know when, if ever again, we'd be bound to each other this way: two women linked and equal by law, their names paratactic on a single page.

Like Mary, we drove to a new metropolis with no place to live, no jobs to report to first thing Monday morning. But we were unlike Mary too, in ways that would come to matter more: we were women not seeking or open to romantic attachments with men.

Angie knew about Mary by then. She had seen the archive, watched the episodes, heard the stories of the way my life tilted on an MTM axis all those years. "Some people just drink to excess," she quipped, but then she was serious. Her eyes were impossibly blue: "Most people have a repressive family, and they rebel. That's what I did. They feel at odds with the world around them, so they lash out, or they self-destruct. But I'm not sure I ever met anyone who—what—recast herself to make her whole world more habitable?"

Speaking of habitable: I had copied verbatim these notes from the MTM set designers:

A ROOM. Actually, an entire apartment, but a single large room. There are some—mostly of the working-girl variety—who would consider this place a "great find": ten-foot ceilings, pegged wood floors, a wood-burning fireplace, and, most important, a fantastic ceiling-height corner window. Right now the room is totally empty, but it won't be for long. It will be the main setting for THE MARY TYLER MOORE SHOW. So God Bless It.

And what were the odds that on our first morning in this unfamiliar city we would come upon a FOR RENT sign in the window of a charming Squirrel Hill apartment building? "It's the third floor," I murmured, like Mary's, and when the man from the realty company came to meet us, we followed him up the stairs and waited as he unlocked the door, and then we entered the enormous empty room and stood beguiled— the high ceilings, the wood floors, the fireplace with its little hearth, and the fantastic atrium in the corner with its tall windows and crystalline doors.

I wrote in my journal: THE MAIN SETTING—we have found it!

THE THIRD INTERVIEW

I walk two miles from our new apartment to the private women's college, and by the time I arrive, the thin white copy of my résumé has wilted in my hands. My hair is wet as if I have gone swimming, and for the rest of the afternoon, sweat continues its steady trickle down my spine.

Humidity: another initiation.

But I take as a good sign that my interview for the position of "Public Safety Secretary" has been scheduled in an old Victorian house with a woman's name: Lindsay House. I would have preferred Mary House, of course, but the job-seeker in the new city cannot be choosy. Her past has been reduced to a soggy lily in her hand, and all her references live in different time zones.

"Are you Julie?" the man in the polo shirt with the Chatham College insignia inquires.

"I am. Are you Bernie?"

He nods and extends his hand. "Boy are we glad to see you!"

I glance around the foyer, but there is no one else there—only Bernie, who wears an empty holster at the hip of his navy Dockers. "Right this way." He holds a door for me, and I step into his sunlit office.

"I'm going to level with you," he says, collapsing with a dramatic sigh into his desk chair. "We're in a bit of a pickle. The school year's about to start, which means the front office is going to be jammed with faculty, staff, and students all trying to purchase their parking permits. We're the campus police department, but we also handle permits—and of course, parking enforcement, meaning tickets, too."

"OK." I am still concerned about the holster at his hip, scanning the room as discreetly as possible for some sign of the missing gun. "I brought my résumé, but I wasn't quite prepared for the heat—"

"Don't worry about it," Bernie says. "I already read what you uploaded to the Human Resources portal. That's why I called you in."

"OK." I nod again. "I feel confident that with a Master's degree in English, I can facilitate whatever paperwork—"

"Sure, sure, sure." He waves his hand as if to say, *Your qualifications don't really concern me.* "It's not a *hard* job exactly. I mean, we only require a high school diploma. The issue is more dealing with the public. It's a customer service kind of thing."

"Well, I have a lot of retail experience, too, and I'm generally pretty patient—"

"I don't know if I made this clear on the phone, but our last Public Safety Secretary *died*." Bernie's pale face is turning mauve now, and I realize that the tone I hear in his voice is not empathy or compassion but undeniable irritation.

"I'm not a superstitious person exactly, but if I didn't know better, I'd say she did it on purpose. Left here in a huff on a Friday afternoon—*early*, I might add—shouting about how I was going to give her a heart attack, and the next thing you know, we get a call that she's died of a heart attack. Took her work keys with her, and no one in her family could find them. Had to break the locks on all the filing cabinets. The whole thing has been a real mess."

"Hmm." I try my best to channel Linda B.'s tranquil face, but my eyes still search for the gun.

"She was a difficult person. We've had a lot of difficult people in this job. We're looking for someone to put a—how can I say this?—a *nicer* face on Public Safety. People mostly come here when they've got a problem, so the person in your position can't *be* the problem, do you see what I'm saying?"

I nod again and smile. Bernie's thin blond hair cannot conceal the way the mauve tides have risen and spread across his head.

"I like that. I bet you're the kind of person who doesn't have to be told to smile. We can use some of that positive energy around here. And you're about to be a graduate student at the University? Is that what I read?"

"Yes. I'm a writer."

"Well, that's terrific because we have a log you'll need to update every day, documenting incidents—criminal, medical, etcetera—that the police officers were called to investigate. Sometimes it's broken air-conditioning units in the dorms or ducks blocking traffic on the road. You can't believe some of the things people report."

He leans back in his chair now, stretches his arms, almost as if he's forgotten I'm here. Then he says, "You know I really like the Seattle area. That's where you're from, right?"

"Yes. It's beautiful—as I'm sure you know."

"Well, I haven't actually *been* out west," he says, "but I got pretty deep into the whole *Twin Peaks* thing in the '90s, and I just love *Frasier*. Those guys are a hoot."

I decide it isn't wise to tell him I've never seen either show, so instead I say, "I'm kind of a classic TV buff myself. I like *Perry Mason* and *Get Smart*—" he's grinning now, as I guessed he would be—"and my favorite of all is *Mary Tyler Moore*."

"*That Girl*, right?" he says, snapping his fingers. "I like her too. Lots of pep. And what was her boyfriend's name?"

It's all I can do to suppress my groan at this unholy comparison. Ann Marie was to Mary as Wonderbread was to stone ground wheat. She was Cool Whip to Mary's real whipped cream, milquetoast to Mary's milkshake fortified with fruit and flax.

"Oh, that's Marlo Thomas actually. Her boyfriend on the show was named Donald, I think."

"Right, right. *Donald!*" Bernie looks pleased, as if we've been discussing an old friend of his. "They were great together." He pauses for a moment, leafs through some papers on his desk, then asks me with a look of fatherly concern: "Did you really move all the way across the country by yourself?"

"No, I—" *I never said I did*—"I moved here with my partner."

Bernie mulls this information over for a minute before he replies. "Well, this job is twenty hours a week, and I'm happy to hire you for it, but only if you're sure you have the time to commit."

"Absolutely! Time management is my strong suit," I pledge with gusto.

"Well, let's hope so—what with graduate school and a whole other business on the side."

"So what did you say after that?" Angie is still unpacking boxes as I stand with my back to the fan and slowly peel off my clothes.

"It took me a minute to really understand that he didn't understand what I meant by *partner*. I said I didn't have a side business, and then he asked me what I had a partner for, so I said *love and companionship*, and then he got all pink again—really flustered, you know—and said he'd show me where the Public Safety Secretary sits."

"Is that really the job title, in 2003?"

"It really is. Says so right on the main door."

"Well, at least there's a bright side," Angie says, grinning at me.

"What's that?"

"You'll be working in your favorite era!"

THE MiGHTY OHiO

The city of Pittsburgh is mentioned only once on *The Mary Tyler Moore Show*, but even that fact is a surprise. The moment is memorable because the city is used as one of the show's most inventive comparisons. Georgette tells Mary that she and Rhoda are "like Pittsburgh," a simile Mary tries to ignore, but her curiosity, like ours, soon enough gets the better of her.

"All right, Georgette. How are Rhoda and I like Pittsburgh?" Georgette goes on to explain that Pittsburgh is the place where the Allegheny River and the Monongahela River meet. By themselves, these are just "two skinny little rivers," but when they come together in Pittsburgh, they form the mighty Ohio River, which is far more powerful than either can be on its own.

"That was my first geography lesson about the mid-Atlantic," I tell Angie as we stand together in Three Rivers Park. "I wrote it down in case I ever happened to be in Pittsburgh."

"And now," she says, with ta-dah hands, "here we are!"

We don't know yet that we're going to make friends in Pittsburgh, or that I'll publish my first poems and essays while we live here, or that Angie will become a librarian. We can't imagine that in another decade, there will be a landmark civil rights case declaring Section 3 of the Defense of Marriage Act unconstitutional, and when that happens, we will become eligible to marry and to receive federal recognition of our marriage. Such things seem unthinkable now.

We don't know yet that Angie's sister is going to have children who will become our niece and nephews, though we do know that aunts are important. Mary Richards' Aunt Flo, played by Eileen Heckart, was one of the women who inspired her to pursue a career in journalism, and then of course Mary went on to inspire Bess not to lose her mind over her mother. Years from now, our niece Evie will announce that she wants to write "stories of other people's lives and also autobiographies."

"Did you know that Mary Tyler Moore's real-life aunt was the one who gave her the famous tam? It wasn't part of the script or anything. She just knew Mary was going to Minneapolis to shoot the opening credits and was worried that she was going to be cold," I tell Angie.

"No, I didn't know," she says, catching on quickly. "But if we ever have a niece, maybe we should give her a tam."

All we know right now is that we are two women alone on a delta. Angie is the Allegheny, and I am the Monongahela, and somehow together we must become the mighty Ohio.

WHAT IS JULIE WADE REALLY LIKE?

Sometimes I find myself standing on a crowded corner in the city, and I want to feel it—that extraordinary surge of freedom and independence that prompted Mary to twirl and toss her tam. But then I think I see my mother in the crowd, and she seizes the day in a different way than the saying intends. I freeze with fear. I fail to cross with the other pedestrians.

Or sometimes I think I see my father in a row of men waiting for the bus, and I want to run up to him and ask if he really believes my life is a sin. Or that woman there, in the café window, who could be my grandmother: I know in my heart I'm never going to see her again. Or that woman there, feeding the meter or feeding the birds: she could be my Aunt Linda, who still has time, I think, to come around.

"You know, your grad school insurance might pay for you to see somebody," Angie suggests.

"Do you think I'm flailing?"

"No, but I think you're struggling more than you have to be. It was a big step telling your parents you wouldn't move home and get help for your—'homosexual tendencies.'" We put a lot of things in air quotes these days because so many words don't feel like our own.

So I find a therapist in Squirrel Hill who mentions "family trauma" and "LGBT" on his list of specialties. I climb the narrow stairs to his office every week. I take some comfort in the fact that his last name is Weise, which when pronounced aloud is indistinguishable from "wise."

After I have been seeing Dr. Weise for several months, he stops me mid-sentence one morning with a gentle splay of his palm: "You know, Julie, you don't have to tell me what you think I want to hear. You can tell me what you think you want to say."

"Do I seem disingenuous to you?" I ask, concerned.

"No. It's more that you seem like you're holding back, not wanting to say the wrong thing or make me uncomfortable in any way."

"I haven't always been like that, believe me. I used to say whatever came into my head."

"Everything? No filter at all?" He looks surprised.

"Well, I mean, not *everything*—and certainly not to *everyone*—but more than I say now."

"What kinds of things didn't you say, growing up?" I notice that Dr. Weise always sits very straight in his chair, and though he sometimes makes notations on his yellow legal pad, he never fidgets. He always seems fully present in the moment at hand.

"Gay things, I guess."

"Like, attraction to other girls?"

I nod, and even though I know I am one of his specialties, I still feel awkward naming it, that thing which has the power to divide us.

"You didn't confide in anyone, even your best friend or your mentor?"

"Well, it's different being an ally than it is being the person who needs the ally. I mean, I didn't even know the word *ally* when I was growing up, but I wanted to be a good person, and I thought that meant being kind and open-minded, like Mary Richards. But if you're an ally, you still hold most of the cards. It's not as vulnerable a position because you're *choosing* to show compassion. I feel vulnerable all the time now because I can't trust who my allies are."

"Can you give me an example?"

"Sure." I shrug. "Every day is an example. I go to work at the Public Safety Office, and there are all these police officers there, and they seem to like me well enough, but they don't know how to talk to me. Heather is young—she's close to my age—and she always tells me about her dating life, and then she says things like 'You wouldn't understand' or 'You don't have to deal with things like that.' And there's this middle-aged officer named Dennis who saw me wearing a tie one day—I always wanted to wear a tie, and I found one I liked at Goodwill, so I wore it with a white button-down shirt and a long corduroy skirt. It made me think of the episode where Mary wears a suit to work on the day she's going to be interviewed about what it's like to be the only woman in the newsroom. Dennis asked, 'So are you wearing that because you're—you know—', and then he couldn't finish the sentence because nothing he was going to say would have been appropriate, and he already has some strikes against him for protocol violations. Finally, after a lot of stammering and throat-clearing, he said, 'Do a lot of women you know dress that way?' I told him, 'Just Mary Richards,' kind of as a joke, and he said, 'Is that your girlfriend?' No one there can even remember Angie's name."

Dr. Weise uncaps his pen, as if he's going to write something down, but then he doesn't. "You know, *I'm* an ally—I mean, I think of myself that way—but you're right about something important I hadn't thought of before. I *do* get to choose to be that way, and I suppose I could choose at any time to be another way. There are different consequences for you, having chosen to be out of the closet. You can't control how other people are going to react." I'm not the best at reading upside down, but I think he sketches *Agency?* on the page.

"I'm struck by the fact that we were talking about ways you might censor yourself or hold back parts of yourself you're concerned aren't pleasing to other people, but the examples you gave are more about other people censoring themselves around *you*, displeasing *you*." It isn't a question, so when I don't reply, he tries again. "What do you think people are missing about you? What is your family missing about you? What is Julie Wade really like?"

I smile at him broadly now. "That's the name of the episode! The one where Mary wears the suit! It's called 'What is Mary Richards Really Like?'"

"If you want," Dr. Weise says—"if it's easier, you can tell me what Mary Richards is like first. Just don't forget that this is your story, so we have to come back to you at the end."

THERE ARE 446 bridges in pittsburgh, and mary richards is one of them

SCENE OPENS with an aerial view of Pittsburgh, taken from Mount Washington. The triangle shape of the city is visible, along with many of the bridges, and prominent in the foreground is the iconic red tram of the Duquesne Incline inching its way up the hill. **CUT TO** a silver station wagon with Washington plates plunging into the Fort Pitt Tunnel as—

(CUE THEME SONG:)
—the iconic MTM opening low blast and echo of a solo trombone, a horn like a big-rig truck, clashes with jazz-trumpet traffic blare. The disconcerting call-and-response followed quickly by a pure, baritone, male vocalist, still youthful, but definitely adult and questioning, backed by soft '70s-style electric guitar and sparse bongo. The lyrics are concerned, worldly, haunted.

CLOSE UP on the faces of two young women in the front seat of that car, as they exit the

(Loose-Leaf Insert)

tunnel, then **PAN OUT** to show the confluence
of the three rivers.

The station wagon heads east on Interstate
376, the electric guitar turns acoustic, melancholy made melodic by the addition of a soft
backup-brass section and riffing sax, passing
the downtown skyscrapers, there's a big world
out there (make note: the PPG building that
looks like a glass castle, crenellated at the
top).

CUT TO the apartment in Squirrel Hill with
the tall windows and the wood floors. Let the
camera **SWEEP PAST** the tiny bedroom in the
back, showing only one bed—cozy with blue
quilt and green blanket—and the wicker IKEA
chair in the corner. The **THEME SONG**'s beat
slowly starts to liven as the lyrics speak of
living—it's time now, and you should know it.
Now the partners are in the kitchen pulling
their first Thanksgiving turkey from the oven.
The brass swells toward a building crescendo.
Love is all around.

They're running together down the steep
slope of Panther Hollow in their summer clothes
(tank tops, shorts)—try to pick up the purple
quality of the heat as the air seems to swaddle
the trees—then transition to the partners
still running but now in their winter clothes
(fleeces, gloves, tights) as they pass through
Schenley Park and alongside the stunning
Phipps Conservatory in sync with brightening
lyrics about giving. Now they're in their work
clothes on the city bus, standing and gazing
out the window as they approach the Cathedral

of Learning. Lyrics soaring, almost light now, as the camera takes in the magnificence of this gothic structure, students and tourists alike flooding the doors—*Carpe diem*—the partners getting coffee at Kiva Han.

EACH PHRASE GUIDES THE TRANSITIONS OF CAMERA SHOTS: to a letter in the mailbox, Julie's key turning the lock, and then her hand reaching inside.

In the final transition, she's running up the stairs outside the Mellon Institute where Angie has just stepped outside. Julie's waving the letter, and we can see that she's been admitted to a PhD program in Louisville. The vocals climax with the instrumentals, trumpets ecstatic now as they embrace at the base of one of those dramatic columns. They can *make it after all*. It's winter, and they're both wearing swing coats. Julie puts her hands into Angie's pockets, and they're kissing, leaning against the column. Then without notice the music fades abruptly behind a sudden xylophone—there it is again, and like an ellipses we're left breathless at those four quick crystal notes. . . .

ANOTHER REUNiON EpisodE

It's the summer of my twenty-ninth year, the biggest brink I've teetered on so far. I wanted to publish a book by the time I was thirty, but that seems unlikely now. The books I write are "atypical," one editor explained. "It's hard to place work that moves all over the place, that keeps no fidelity to any one genre." Another said simply: "You ask more than many readers are willing to give."

It's summer, and Angie wants to take a long-overdue vacation. "Why not Seattle?" she asks. "We fell in love out there, our grad school friends are there, and who could dispute the beauty of the Emerald City in summertime?"

I send April a message when we land, and she replies,

Hello from Vegas!

It's the kind of sparkly place she loves: cabarets and craps tables, massages and mimosas, then a chaise lounge by the pool with cucumbers over her eyes.

Hello from Seattle!

OMG! Are you there right now?

I am.

> I can't believe we're missing each other again!

I think but don't type: *I can*. It seems we've been missing each other less and less, which is why we've been missing each other more and more. This paradox brings me no pleasure.

Later I send a picture of a cocktail glass with a polka dot umbrella in it:

> Have a terrific vacation! You deserve it.

Over the years my parents and I have exchanged some difficult correspondences, but one fact looms above all else: they do not want to see me as I am. My mother knows "lesbians make themselves ugly for each other," and if I ever come home, she insists I must come alone.

So maybe I am mother-less now? Is twenty-nine too old to be an orphan?

I write to Linda B. next:

> Would you like to have lunch while I'm in town? Maybe we could meet up at the Pegasus Pizza on Alki Beach—you know, for old times' sake.

She sends me a heart and a smiley face emoji, then agrees to pick me up at the water taxi station. I'll be traveling across the harbor from downtown.

This time we order wine and clink our glasses together. The waitress smiles at us and says, "I just love it when old friends get together for lunch."

"Are we old friends now?" It hadn't occurred to me that one day Linda B. and I would be grown-ups at the same time.

"Maybe we are. So, tell me, Old Friend, how have you been?"

"I don't know. A little antsy, I guess. Somebody told me once in college that your twenties are just the staging area for your thirties. Do you think that's true?"

Linda is her usual serene self. She takes time to reflect on the question before positing an answer. "Well, not any more than I think your thirties are a staging area for your forties, or your forties for your fifties. There's a strange kind of momentum to this life: the longer you live, the faster it goes. And that run-away train feeling—"

"Nice image," I commend.

"Thank you," and she bows a little in her chair. "That feeling can give you a false sense that everything is riding on the moment at hand, that everything has been building and building and now something monumental *has* to happen—or the world just might end."

We both laugh, and then I say, "You know what's crazy?"

"Hmm?"

"I am the age you were when I first met you."

Linda's golden brows arch, and she gestures toward me. "I was *this* age when you met me?"

"Yup. You were twenty-nine. I intercepted you in your front yard—"

"Oh, I remember *that*," she smiles, "and I was twenty-nine when I bought that house, but—wow. You're really twenty-nine now?"

I nod. "And the thing is, I wish I had thought to ask you then what twenty-nine felt like because I feel so *different* from how I thought I'd feel at this age."

"Well, I think the obvious question is—*how did you think you'd feel?*"

"Like a grown-up!" I say it a little too loudly, so then I lean in and whisper: "I mean, I had my height by the time I started high school, and I just read that our brains are fully baked by the time we're twenty-two, twenty-three, tops. So why do I feel so astonished all the time, when I'm paying a bill or following a recipe or trying to fit that stupid Swiffer WetJet refill bottle into the socket?"

Linda laughs. "We've all been there."

"But it's like I can't believe it's me who's doing these things, and I keep wondering when it's going to stop feeling like I'm *acting* like an adult and I just *am* one."

"Well, you know those actors who star in a long-running Broadway play? I mean, the kind of play that sells out years in advance, so they've got the part every day in relative perpetuity?"

"Sure."

"Well, if we don't die young—I mean, barring some tragic accident—we *are* those actors, in a sense. We're playing the part of an adult every day in relative perpetuity. I think we can only grow deeper into it, keep finding more nuances in the role."

"That's smart," I say, nodding. "That gives me hope actually. And somebody gave Angie a book when she turned thirty that says your thirties are the decade when you're least likely to die. So that's—you know—ideally—more playing time."

"How is Angie? Am I ever going to get to meet her?"

"Sure, you will. She had something else to do today, and she thought I should have this time for our reunion." I like that Linda asks about the woman I love without hesitation. "Speaking of which: how's Paul? How's Ellen?"

"Oh, they're good. Paul's flying to Alaska today for work, and Ellen"—Linda checks her watch—"Ellen gets out of day camp in about half an hour. I was hoping you'd want to ride along with me and meet her."

"Sure, yeah. She must be—" I work the math in my head—"eight years old by now?" Another only child—only daughter—growing up in Fauntlee Hills.

"That's right. Starting third grade in the fall." Linda looks down at her plate, pauses before she says: "You know, there are more kids in the neighborhood these days. Not a lot, but certainly more than when you and April lived there, and I think the mores are changing some—*loosening*."

"Well, that's good. I'm glad to hear it."

"One of Ellen's best friends lives next door to your parents, actually, so I see them working out in the yard from time to time. I've never mentioned that you and I are still in touch, but I've wondered—if *you're* in touch with them." Linda meets my eyes now: "You can feel free to tell me it's none of my business, but I knew they didn't take your coming out well, and—I guess I hoped they had revised some of their earlier opinions."

I don't expect it to be so hard talking about my parents. I've had a lot of practice in therapy, and I know we don't have long before I'll need to put on my happy face to meet Linda's little girl. I say, "So I have to mention Mary, of course. I've waited as long as I could."

We both smile, and Linda pours us each some more wine.

"I guess maybe when you were single and—before you got serious with Paul—well, I wasn't paying that much attention to how it must have been for you, but I see now there was probably pressure from the larger world to get married, to have kids, to conform to other people's expectations about when and how you should do those things. I mean, there were probably people who thought you shouldn't buy a house on your own, that you should have waited until you had a husband."

Linda nods. "That's true. There were. No small number of them either."

"On the show, Phyllis tells Mary 'I want to see you married, Mary, because *I'm* married,' which is more explicit than most people are about their motives. I thought I knew how it would be, you know, from watching *Mary Tyler Moore* for so many years. I had a sense of the kind of presumptions and prescriptions people make for other people's lives, particularly young women's lives, and I remembered all the things you taught me about keeping my own truth in sight. Granted, I could have come out sooner, but once I did, you know, I really *came out*— to everyone—and I'm not willing to go back in."

Maybe what I see in Linda's face is admiration now. Maybe she is mirroring for me the way I have looked at her all these years.

"But—there are two things Mary Richards didn't have to face that I do. She didn't have to brace herself for homophobia all the time. She didn't have to actually *disappoint* people, or *sicken* them, or *enrage* them—and you can see it happen, the way their bodies shift and their eyes avert—by telling them that she was gay. See, people want me to get married and have babies, too, but they want that life for me *in lieu of* the life I already have. People—not all people, but a lot of people—want to strike right through me, cross out everything I've written all these years."

Linda is nodding. She doesn't know what to say, and I can't help her with her lines. I can barely muddle through mine.

"And the other thing Mary Richards doesn't know about, that *I* didn't know about, is how much other people want you to be close to your parents. They've got such a stake in it. I don't know why. Maybe even more than the marriage and the babies. And I don't mean you when I say this, Linda. You were there. You saw how it all went down for me. But I mean all the people who don't know my past, some of whom really mean well, but they just don't want to let this go. It's some version of *I want to see you have a close relationship with your parents, Julie, because I have a close relationship with mine*. They want to make sure I feel bad about the relationship I don't have with my parents so that I'll work harder to repair it. But the truth is, I don't think it can be repaired. I saw a therapist in Pittsburgh for a good long while, and he didn't think it could be repaired either."

At just this moment, the waitress stops by to ask if we'd like anything else. "Oh, looks like things got real serious here." I have tears in my eyes, and though Linda is wearing her glasses again, I can see tears welling up in hers.

"We'll take the check," she says, and when it comes, she reaches for the black padded folder. Linda signals that our conversation will continue; that this is only an intermission: "You get the next one, OK?"

MIAMI IS MY TIPPERARY

It's a long way to Tipperary,
It's a long way to go.
It's a long way to little Mary
To the sweetest girl I know!
Goodbye, Piccadilly,
Farewell, Leicester Square!
It's a long long way to Tipperary,
But my heart's right there.

THE MARY YEARS

In my thirtieth year, Mary Tyler Moore turns seventy-three, the inverse of her symbolic thirty-seven. She publishes a second autobiography titled *Growing Up Again*, and the phrase blossoms as I turn it over on my tongue. What is there to do but grow up again—and again? In this cyclical world, we keep finding ourselves at new starting lines, no matter how far into the distance we have already run.

Consider that I began watching *The Mary Tyler Moore Show* and reading the Mary Tyler Moore story nearly two decades before. Consider that I have carried these women like two halves of the same heart alongside my own heart all these years. Consider that the heart is heavy. Even when it is light, the heart is heavy.

Consider that, at the conclusion of the series to which she had given her name, Mary Tyler Moore teetered on the brink of becoming Mary Richards—single (after her second divorce), childless (after the death of her son)—a shadow-version of the woman she had spent so many years portraying, now a decade older and steeped in deeper griefs. It was another starting line, and this time she would have to run toward the future knowing precisely what she had lost.

Consider that, at the conclusion of my proto Mary years, these words from Mary Tyler Moore were posted on my bulletin board, included in my email signature line: **"I'm not so fearful anymore. I've already seen the darkness."**

MTM had seen more darkness than MR, for all her empathy and compassion, could have imagined. I wondered if there were times she envied the character that she had played.

SEASON HIGHLIGHTS: AGE 30

Since Pittsburgh was my Minneapolis, I drove back for the celebration and invocation of my Mary years. It was both, of course. My beloved came with me, of course. This was a pilgrimage to kneel on old turf and draw a new starting line in the pliable earth.

At this time, in theaters everywhere, a film called *Julie & Julia* is playing. It's a classic juxtaposition story, the twining of two women's lives. And to my great delight, the narrative is nonfiction. Julie Powell wrote a memoir subtitled *My Year of Cooking Dangerously* in which she endeavored to cook—in 365 days in a tiny New York apartment—all 524 of Julia Child's recipes from *Mastering the Art of French Cooking.*

Angie and I buy our tickets online to ensure they won't sell out. She enjoys the film well enough, but I am enraptured. "A name is a door!" I declare as we step out into the warm September air. It's my birthday eve, when I've been known to wax poetic or simply ramble. "I love the way Julia Child, without ever knowing it, props open the door for another Julie in a future place and time!"

Angie kisses my cheek in the car. "Maybe someday you'll write the memoir that braids your life with Mary's."

Here's the part that sounds like a fairy tale, almost too serendipitous to believe. On my thirtieth birthday, Angie and I are wandering through Phipps Conservatory, one of our favorite places on earth. Perhaps it is an enchanted garden after all.

Sunlight streams decadently through the windows. In one room, butterflies alight on our shoulders and hands.

When I stop to retrieve my bag from the locker in the lobby, my cell phone reports one missed call and a message. We sit on a bench outside, drenched in that same decadent sunlight, as a new voice spills into my ear: "Yes, I'm trying to reach Julie Marie Wade. This is Sarah Gorham from Sarabande Books. I'm calling in regards to the manuscript you sent us some months back." She leaves her number and asks me to call—the editor-in-chief of my favorite press.

There is a photograph of the moment just after, when I've dialed the number and am listening to the woman on the other end of the line tell me that she is going to publish my book. I don't remember Angie taking the picture. I can't imagine how she found the wherewithal to document this moment that had given *momentous* its name. But I'm struck most by how young I look for thirty, how novice to be talking contracts and time-lines with a publisher who doesn't even know it's my birthday as she is giving me this most extraordinary gift.

Neither Mary is mentioned in my memoir, but I live in a sub-junctive mood after all, where both have underwritten every line.

SEASON HIGHLIGHTS: AGE 31

Remember the episode where we learn (it shocked me as a teen) that Mary lied on her résumé about having a college degree? This is one of the secrets our heroine hides in that capacious closet of hers, and Rhoda, who keeps secrets poorly and makes no secret of this fact, outs her friend to everyone in the news-room. The revelation causes Mary much shame and dismay—in part because she only completed two years of college and in part, perhaps in larger part, because she was caught in a lie.

For viewers, the revelation reminds us of Mary's vulnerability, her essential humanity. Like us, she sometimes overcompensates, second-guesses herself, doubts that she will really make it on her own.

I thought about this plot point a lot in relation to my friend April. She never graduated from college either, and in many ways, her Mary Richards years resembled Mary's more than mine did. April had her own apartment, worked at a retail job downtown, and if Facebook was any indication, seemed to enjoy plenty of leisure time going on dates and out with friends from work. In all her posted snapshots, she was beaming, well-dressed and pretty and popular.

By my own thirty-first year, I had completed three degrees, and only one semester of coursework remained for my fourth. After that, the multi-lane highway of scholarly exploration narrowed to a single road: comprehensive exams, followed by dissertation preparation and defense, followed by the academic job market. Then the road would fork dramatically. One route led toward unemployment or underemployment, years of working "outside the field" or "beside the field" while interviewing for positions "within." It was a painful version of nearby. We all knew people who had earned their doctorates only to begin adjuncting for multiple schools while managing their neighborhood Starbucks, struggling to pay down ever-compounding student debt. We all knew we could easily become them.

The other route was the coveted one but daunting nonetheless: a tenure-track career at a single institution, a lifetime on the other side of the desk.

Angie and I were driving across town discussing this very conundrum—the way the long pursuit of a particular destination can become more frightening as its proximity nears. You're so close, but you feel so far. Then you get closer still, and as the longing grows, so does the fear that courts it. You want to cover your eyes, but at the same time, you can't bear the thought of missing it; neither can you bear the thought of meeting it head on.

Suddenly, she switched lanes and said, "Let's go see Carol."

Carol was Mary Richards at 50 with a rock-and-roll band. Carol was Mary Richards with three dogs and a pick-up truck and a funky old house in the Highlands. Carol was Mary Richards on her third career, revving the engine for her own final showdown with those comprehensive exams.

This part, too, sounds like a fairy tale, but I promise it's true: When she opens the door, Carol is not alone in her funky old house with her collection of globes and her books water-falling from slanted shelves. No, tonight she is accompanied by everyone we know—peers and professors, neighbors and friends—and there where the dining room table once stood is the band. A name has proven too hard to choose, so they go by "That Band." The placeholder title stuck like super glue.

Matt, a semiotician who styles hair for a living and writes songs on the side, is working the snare drums with a soft, steady beat. Elijah, the philosopher who studies autodidacts like Rafinesque, strums his acoustic guitar. As everyone is shouting "Surprise!" and "Happy birthday!" he leans into the mike and begins to croon—yes, *croon*—a song he has learned by ear only yesterday, listening to crackly YouTube uploads: *"Who can turn the world on with her smile? . . ."*

Soon everyone is clapping and singing along as the song crescendos to its glorious promise and premonition.

"They chose the second season lyrics," I whisper to Angie, "the ones that sound so much more certain about everything."

"Well," she whispers back, "this is your second season."

I am still wiping my eyes when Carol, who is an art therapist and a caterer turned drama teacher and Humanities scholar, says, "May I interest you in a Brandy Alexander?"

The tears resume, and I nod and cry all the way into her kitchen where she places the cocktail, which I have never tasted until this night, into my trembling hand. And for a moment, everything is absolutely right with the world.

SEASON HIGHLIGHTS: AGE 32

Now let's return to the second half of that episode where we learn that Mary has lied on her résumé. After some inevitable ribbing, Mr. Grant escorts Mary ("if that's even your real name") into his office and explains that he didn't hire her because he thought she had a college degree. This rings true to the viewer at home. After all, we remember how it began. We were there, watching Mary hand him the sheet of paper, watching him peruse it casually as he offered her a drink. We laughed when she asked for a Brandy Alexander, then again when he was forced to offer coffee instead.

We all thought Lou hired Mary for her spunk, even though he claimed he hated it.

But here we are, several years deep in the series, and Lou reveals something that happened outside our purview: "I hired you because on your way into my office, you bumped into a desk and said excuse me. I thought, *There must be something special about a person who's kind to an inanimate object.*"

I was touched by that scene the many times I had seen it until, as a thirty-two-year-old woman with a newly minted Ph.D., I went out on the job market hoping to be hired for my credentials, not for how nice I could be to a piece of furniture.

During my first interview of the new era, I sat in a hotel desk chair while two faculty members reclined against the headboard of a bed and the third perched awkwardly on the radiator. They each held a clipboard and took turns asking questions from a standardized list. "This is for the EEOC," one woman on the bed explained. "We have to ask each job candidate the same questions in the same order, so please excuse any redundancies or non sequiturs."

I recited my strengths and weaknesses; I imagined myself into difficult teaching scenarios; I described my writing practice and plans for future publication. Everyone was cordial and pro-fessional, but there was no spark. When the timer rang and I exited the room, I could not even recall their names. I doubted by the end of the day that any one of them would recall mine.

On another interview, I was flown to a college in eastern Pennsylvania during a light snowstorm. I wore my Mary Richards-inspired boots and coat, and I rode the long distance from the airport in a town car driven by a man in a leather cap.

"Do you mind my asking what you're interviewing for?"

"It's a professorship," I said, "at the college. If I get this job, I'll teach poetry and creative nonfiction for a living."

He eyed me in the mirror. "No offense, but you look a little young for a job like that. Aren't professors supposed to have elbow pads and silver temples and walk around muttering to themselves?"

"Well, give me time. We have to grow into our foibles, I think. Or maybe we just have to earn the right to show them."

The snow was coming down harder by then, but softer too, those big storybook flakes I associate with *It's a Wonderful Life* and scene transitions from *Mary Tyler Moore*. The driver had been instructed to drop me off at a bed and breakfast on the outskirts of town, where I'd check in and have a couple of hours to relax and freshen up before the official campus interview began.

"Good luck!" he offered, tapping his cap and placing my suitcase on the wooden porch beneath the eaves. A steady curtain of snow surrounded me on all sides as I knocked on the door and attempted to peer through the lacy curtains. That's when I noticed a sign taped to the window:

B & B IS CLOSED BETWEEN 12 AND 2 DAILY. CHECK-INS PLEASE RETURN AT AN APPROPRIATE TIME.

I slid up my sleeve: 12:05, the watch-face read.

First, I stood and gazed out at the road: No sidewalks. Cars were beginning to skid. It was a two-lane highway with rusted guardrails; beyond them, miles of newly flocked firs.

Next, I paced the length of the porch, rubbed my hands together, wondered what Mary Richards would do in my shoes. *Maybe this is part of the interview? Maybe there's a camera in that Christmas cactus that's recording me now. Am I patient enough? Am I rugged enough? Do I have the kind of stamina a job like this will require? And am I kind, most importantly, to the flower pots and the wind chimes and even the doormat that proclaims its dubious WELCOME?*

At 2 PM sharp, when the student worker arrived to unlock the door, he was plainly shocked to see me there: a young woman perched on her suitcase, a book splayed open on her lap, and her ears nearly as red as the lone fire hydrant at the foot of the drive. No wonder Mary Richards wore a hat.

But in fairy tales as in television and sometimes in real life, magic belongs to the province of threes. We don't know how many jobs Mary Richards called about before she came to Minneapolis—and remember, the original secretarial position at WJM had already been filled before she arrived.

A few weeks later I'm waiting in the lobby of the Palmer House in Chicago, a hotel so fancy I'm certain I don't belong. That's when I see them, though they don't see me: the faculty who are here to interview me for this job. They've just flown in from Florida, and they don't know how to dress for the cold: sneakers instead of boots; hoodies instead of coats. They look ragtag and rumpled with wind-burned faces, but they are animated too—three men talking with their hands.

When I'm summoned to the suite, I find no clipboards. John sits sideways in his chair, thumps the packet of papers on his lap. "It's your application," he says. "Lots of good stuff in here." I love the Massachusetts in his voice, the snowy-white wonder of his hair.

Les is fiddling with the thermostat, and Campbell is filling a pitcher with water, and someone calls out, "By the way, we do have women in our department! You wouldn't be the only one!"

I nod. I'm familiar with the faculty. In fact, my favorite poet teaches there. For months, since I saw the job post, but truthfully long before, I'd been dreaming of Miami, doodling palm trees in the margins of every draft. It's dangerous, I know, to want something so much, to yearn for this job the way I once yearned for that autographed picture of Mary Tyler Moore.

"Before we get started, can we offer you something to drink? Water? Coffee?"

Their faces are open as envelopes, their lips unclasped and smiling. "I'll have a Brandy Alexander," I quip. And before I can add "Just kidding," I hear John laugh.

"Nice one. Mary Tyler Moore." He nods, and we all settle a little deeper into our chairs. I'm at ease here in their presence, surprised by how naturally we fall into conversation. And John's words linger in the air, as if he had dubbed me ceremoniously: "Nice one, *Mary Tyler Moore*."

DRAMATIS PERSONAE

DIRECTOR'S NOTE: I don't expect them to be my family. I'm not looking for a replica of WJM anymore. Yet I have the strangest feeling, sitting in that hotel suite in Chicago, and later on my campus visit in Miami, that I belong in their company, that I should be cast. And wasn't it worth noting that no creative writing faculty member had ever left the program except to retire? What was the secret of their longevity, alone and together?

LYNNE B: I learn that Lynne has an only child, a son who is gay like me. I learn it is possible for a parent to celebrate her child's life and truth without wishing him otherwise. Once, years before I joined the faculty, Lynne was in a car wreck on a desolate road, where she sustained significant damage to her right, formerly dominant hand. After many surgeries, resulting in a scar that merged with her palm lines to form an intricate map, Lynne taught herself to write using her left hand. Surely this was another version of making it after all.

CINDY C: I learn Cindy and John fell in love in graduate school, much the way Angie and I did. Their marriage has endured for more than 30 years, and there is no sense of "sticking it out," no sense of "too proud to call it quits." I love their love story. I love that Cindy is a small woman with an enormous presence, who will not be reconfigured by anyone into a puppet or a doll. Sometimes she wears a shirt that reads Woman Next Door. Sometimes she intimidates the men who usually intimidate the women at Home Depot. I love that she leaves books in my mailbox that she knows I will savor, like Katie Ford's *Blood Lyrics* and Ocean Vuong's *Night Sky with Exit Wounds*.

DEBRA D: Like me, Debra is from Seattle. What are the odds of meeting another Pacific Northwesterner here on the Southeastern Coast? Like me, she loves the ocean, the salt wind in her hair, the immense pleasure of taking a good book to the beach. Like me, she never wanted children, which forges a bond between women who have so often been told that they "should," that they "must." Once, Debra revealed that she and her husband Cliff sometimes watch *The Dick Van Dyke Show* before bed. This fact delighted me, prompting Debra to say: "You know, not every young person would be comfortable joining a faculty where everyone is so much older. Yet here you are, twenty years younger than the youngest of us, and somehow that generation gap hasn't even appeared." Which prompted me to say, and in saying to realize: "Where I come from, I was always the youngest one. I've always been happiest looking up."

JOHN D: Most weeks I go walking with John. We start beside the gnarled mangroves, then past the pub we love and over the drawbridge. The middle miles we walk by the shore. John and I have an easy chemistry. We are united by a love of cats and words, gossip and the Oxford comma, of course—not to mention our singular love for singular women, the one woman without whom our own lives would cease to make sense. In John, I recognize an immense capacity for devotion. I have it too. What I lack in fidelity to genre I manifest in fidelity to people, to vocation. But what if I were not a "known lesbian"? Would I be able to take long walks with an older man and not arouse the suspicions of our friends, neighbors, colleagues? I suspect a friendship like ours would not be possible without the freedom from speculation my orientation provides.

DENISE D: Years ago, Denise wrote a poem that captured my heart and my imagination called "When I Was a Lesbian." I went on to read everything she had ever written and wrote once in my journal that surely Denise was the Mary Richards of poetry for me, the one in whose literary footsteps I most wanted to follow. I didn't have to worry that Denise might harbor a secret homophobia or wonder if she had ever formed a close friendship with a woman who was gay. Denise wrote brilliant collaborations with an extraordinary lesbian poet named Maureen Seaton. Like Mary and me, Denise turned out to be a smiley, cheerful person in real life. We could talk about anything, including the fact that people often mistook our cheerfulness as a sign of ignorance, even stupidity. After all, why would you go around smiling all the time unless you were too daft to realize that everything was terrible? I wondered if this was how Mary felt sometimes, both the character and the actor: that people underestimated her intelligence because she was inclined to look for the light, and when necessary, to become it.

CAMPBELL M: I read Campbell's *American Noise* when Angie and I first drove east across the country from Seattle to Pittsburgh. Then I read his *Florida Poems* as Angie and I traveled south and prepared to plant ourselves anew in the Sunshine State. Here was a poet who made challenges for himself on the page, not trouble in the world for other people. During my first year teaching in the program, I left a copy of a new publication in all my colleagues' mailboxes. It was meant as a gift—no reply required—but I remember how Campbell came into my office, sat across the desk from me, and asked questions. He was curious, genuinely so. He had read what I wrote and wanted to engage in a conversation about it. This was what they meant by "collegiality," wasn't it? This was what they meant by "goodness of fit"?

LES S: Les directs the program in creative writing. He has done so since 1981. When he picked me up at the airport for our interview, the first thing we did was drive around South Florida—everywhere he could think to take me: Miami Beach, Brickell, the Biltmore Hotel, Coral Gables, Coconut Grove, and finally to the Biscayne Bay Campus where I would give my job talk and meet my future students. It wasn't like any interview I had experienced before. We were just talking, almost like old friends, and I told him I had a partner, and he asked, without missing a beat, "What does she do?" He wasn't confused about our relationship or unsettled by it. And when he revealed that he had gone to Muskingum College in Ohio, I said, without missing a beat, "Isn't that where Agnes Moorehead went to school?" Les looked at me like I had secret powers. "It is! But how in the world do you know that?" I worried he might not return his eyes to the road. "How in the world do you even know who Agnes Moorehead is?!"

SEASON HIGHLIGHTS: AGE 33

Mary Tyler Moore was thirty-three the year *The Mary Tyler Moore Show* premiered on television. Christians I knew called it "the Messianic year" because Jesus was 33 at the time of his Crucifixion and Resurrection. That life and death stuff was rough, to be sure, but Mary's return to television couldn't have been easy either.

The show's producers were worried that viewers would have trouble separating Mary Richards from Laura Petrie. Mary herself must have worried about "making it on her own" without Dick Van Dyke by her side. They looked so good together on screen, so seamless in their depiction of a husband and wife who loved each other madly and knew their way around a song and dance. Their son Ritchie had always seemed an afterthought to me, like maybe the producers of that show worried that viewers wouldn't accept a happily married couple without a child.

Laura Petrie had one son named Ritchie. Mary Tyler Moore had one son named Richie. The spelling was different, but I wondered if the name choice was a subtle homage. The two boys would have even been about the same age, and names, as we know, are a way of carrying someone with us.

When I was thirty-three, I began a tenure-track job at a Research One university, knowing much would be expected of me. Christians I knew said this was always the case when much had been given to someone. It seemed such a great leap to begin working with graduate students on their book-length manuscripts when, at thirty-two, I had still been a graduate student myself, just finishing a dissertation of my own.

"But remember," Angie said, "they don't know you as the student you were. They know you as the teacher you are now, as the teacher you'll be for them. It's not like Laura Petrie. They didn't watch you on another series first."

A little joke, in the spirit of Rhoda: "What's the difference between a fresh start and a trial by fire? (Do you give up?) Smoke."

Before my first class, I smoked a cigarette, something I hadn't done in years. I learned to flick a lighter when Nancy at Lamonts let me light cigarettes for her on the loading dock. She took deep drags and cautioned between them: "Make sure you never start this shit."

On *The Dick Van Dyke Show*, everyone smoked. It wasn't a big deal. The cigarettes seemed natural, elegant without being contrived. A decade later, on *The Mary Tyler Moore Show*, no one smoked. It would have been a different show—grittier, grimier somehow—if anyone had. Maybe this was how mores always changed: slowly, by the power of omission. First, we stop looking for it, and eventually we don't even notice the thing that isn't there.

In 1991, *Nick at Nite* released *The Dick Van Dyke Show*, and then *The Mary Tyler Moore Show* the following year. I was already primed to receive them, already watching everything that aired on that singular blast-from-the-past station, yet it took several weeks before I realized the two female leads were played by the same person.

"Dad!" I called him into the room, feeling proud but incredulous, too, like I had just solved a caper but didn't yet believe what I had learned. "The voiceover says *Mary Tyler Moore* right before her husband trips over the hassock—" that's what we called it in our house, a hassock—"and then that's the same name the screen shows right before we see her in the car."

My father laughed. "Well, no kidding, Smidge! First she starred on his show, and then she did so well she got her own show after. That's called working your way up.

This memory returns to me in the Publix parking lot, where I'm smoking an American Spirit before I minty-fresh myself and drive to school. *How had I forgotten something like that?* Even after my dad confirmed they were the same person, I refused to accept *The Dick Van Dyke Show* came first.

"Just look, Dad. She's obviously older there. She's all grown up," I said, pointing to Laura Petrie. Her figure looked fuller to me, and her voice sounded deeper, perhaps from all that smoking. (Kent cigarettes were a sponsor of the show.) Everything about her, from her wardrobe to the way she moved to the way she spoke, made her seem older to me than her alter ego.

And now here I was, in my thirties, smoking like a twenty-something in my car, feeling younger and less prepared than ever. Perhaps I needed to channel my inner Laura Petrie, the woman who *seemed* older, who came across as confident and poised. (And Laura wasn't known for her disastrous dinner parties either...) I stubbed out my cigarette and started the engine. I would walk into that seminar room, smile at everyone, and do my best not to burn anything down.

Late in the year, I'm talking with some students after class. This ritual now feels as natural as stars lighting up on 1960s television. One student asks, "Did you always know you wanted to be a writer when you grew up?"

I nod. "The writing part was always a given for me, but not the teaching. I didn't have any idea about teaching until I was granted a fellowship in my twenties."

"So what did you think you were going to do—you know, to earn a living?"

They are looking at me with such anticipation, waiting for me to pass down a piece of my own story, which might somehow be useful to them as they continue assembling theirs. And how can I deny them anything, my students, when I have spent my whole life with a tiny Steno pad in hand, a pencil tucked behind my ear?

"Well, my parents wanted me to be a doctor—the medical kind—and I wanted to be a private detective or a spy."

"Really?"

"Really."

"Your parents are probably proud of you anyway, right? I mean, you have a good job, and people call you doctor sometimes."

"Let's put it this way: Me not going to med school is *not* the most disappointing thing my parents have had to face."

They laugh, but I can't tell if they know what I'm really getting at. Some part of me doesn't want them to know.

"Well, are you ever sad you don't get to solve mysteries as your job?"

"Who says I don't?" We're standing in the breezeway, and I can smell jasmine flowers now and also salt from the Bay. "Everything we read, everything we write—all of it turns out to be an ongoing investigation—into the world and into ourselves."

On the last day, one of those students brings doughnuts and coffee to share. "To fortify us for the stakeout," she grins at me.

SEASON HIGHLIGHTS: AGE 34

When my mother was thirty-four, she had a daughter. People were always asking her, "What took you so long?" She didn't want to say, "Cancer." She didn't want to say, "Heartache." She didn't want to say, "For the longest time, I feared I would never get what I wanted most."

I never wanted to say to my mother, "See? You still didn't." But my actions spoke for me.

When I was thirty-four, the laws changed, and a door long closed, padlocked even, suddenly came ajar. "Marry me?" I asked Angie. "Marry me?" she asked me. We planned a small ceremony at an old haunt, a place we used to frequent in grad school.

That's when I sent a letter to my parents. I told them I was stepping off the page into a story I never expected to inhabit. Marriage was not for people like me, for lives like mine. But then, just as suddenly, it was.

Before Angie and I left for Washington, a graduate student stopped by my office. "I wanted to give you something for your wedding," Jan said. "There's a scarf I knitted for Angie, because I know it's going to be cold there. And for you—" she made a grand gesture—"it seemed only fitting that I should knit you the Mary Richards tam."

There it was, in my hand, what could have been mistaken for the original artifact: all the same colors, the perfect patterning of blue and black and green. "Jan! I don't know what to say! Maybe for the first time in my whole life—I don't know what to say!"

"Say you'll wear it in good health and toss it every chance you get." I slip the tam onto my head, slant it at a jaunty angle. "See?" Jan says, mirroring my grin. "It's your Mary/merry/marry tam. Any way you say it is true."

Jan is older than I am. She has already lived through her Mary years and proceeds in the world with empathy and compassion. I bet she has hugged and mended some furniture in her day.

I tell Jan the story of Mary Tyler Moore's aunt, wanting her to be warm in the Midwest. "She didn't make the tam, though. She bought it for Mary. And Mary loved it so much that she kept it all those years. Then after her divorce Mary moved back to New York City, and it was stolen from her storage locker."

Jan gapes at me. "You mean, nobody knows what happened to the tam? I just figured it must be in a museum or something."

I shake my head. "Julie!" Jan exclaims. "This is the mystery you've been called to solve."

It snowed on my wedding day and I wore the tam. My parents never wrote back.

SEASON HIGHLIGHTS: AGE 35

When I am thirty-five, I fall hard. Most of my falls have been hard, it's true, but most of my falls have also been metaphors: falling in love, falling from grace, falling asleep or in line or out of fashion. I fall all the time.

But this is what they mean by "slip and fall" on billboards at bus stops and during commercials on live TV. Nothing metaphorical about it. I slip on a flooded tile floor. I fall over a ledge, land upright like the letter L. A shattering sound followed by a more alarming silence. Something inside me has severed.

I tell the paramedics the Miami Book Fair is tomorrow, that I'm scheduled to read with Roger Reeves. "Superman?" one of the young men asks, skeptical.

"In a way," I say. "He's a poet of prodigious abilities."

"I'm afraid you may have to sit this one out," another says as he scoops me up on the board, then lays me flat on the stretcher. His metaphor has a dingy, literal cast to it, and for the first time since falling, I cringe.

"Are you in pain, ma'am?"

"Not physically, no."

I am not thinking of Mary now, my faithful touchstone when traveling an unfamiliar path. I am not thinking of Mary at all. Angie is holding my hand over the silver rail of the hospital bed, and soon our friends John and Cindy appear.

"What a way to spend a Friday night!" I say, and then we are chatting as if nothing is wrong, as if this room is a perfectly natural place for us to gather. I keep asking John for a coffee, and he keeps saying it might interfere with the morphine, and then a woman comes in wearing the telltale white coat with a stethoscope around her neck, and I giggle—the morphine riding through my veins like a trolley car—"I'm a doctor too," I tell her proudly.

"Is that a fact?"

"Ph.D.," Angie clarifies.

"Which means I'm better at metaphors than real life!"

"I see. Well, I find it remarkable that you broke both leg bones and came to us smiling. Most people would have come to us screaming."

"It didn't hurt," I say. "*Really*." The morphine was just to numb me for a series of X-rays.

"Be that as it may," she says, "I'm getting the feeling you're one of those glass-half-full kind of people. Life gives you lemons, you make—"

"Lemon bars!" I beam. And now, for just a moment before they wheel me away, I think of Mary— the way I didn't have to think of Mary to find her manifest within me, like the secular saint she was.

"I still want to read with Roger Reeves tomorrow!" My voice is close, but my body feels very far away.

First there is a cast, but not the kind that anyone can sign. Then there is a surgery, followed by a blue vinyl wheelchair on loan from Campus Health. For a few weeks, I get to take a turn as Ironside. I tell my students I'm out to crack the case, but no one seems to catch the reference.

"Raymond Burr?—Anyone?—*Bueller?*" Can it be they don't recognize the second reference either?

Then there are crutches and a walking boot. John takes me to pick it up at a strange warehouse space called Hanger Prosthetics. The way Mary and Lou would do, no doubt, we stop for Jackson's famous chocolate milkshakes on the way home.

Then physical therapy: weeks and weeks of trying to climb "the stairs to nowhere": three on one side, then a landing, then three on the other side. I try to pretend I'm looking out the window at something grand, but it's just a Subway and the biggest speed bump in the strip mall parking lot.

"You can take this at your own pace," Chad says. "Recovery is never a race."

"Oh, but it is, in my case. I've got Minneapolis in just one month."

Even more than the Miami Book Fair, I was looking forward to this writers' conference in the Mary Richards city. I'd had it starred on my calendar for over a year.

"Minneapolis, huh? Never been. What's so special about it?"

"It's the city where *The Mary Tyler Moore Show* was set."

He shrugged. "Never heard of it."

Chad was older than I was but not by much. Sometimes I forgot that I was older than I was, too.

"And you're going to be doing a lot of walking there?"

"All around the famous lake of course, then all the way to Mary's apartment house."

Chad nods and holds my ankle steady. He wants me to practice putting all my weight into my left foot again. "It's good to have a goal," he says, "so I'm going to pretend that I have some idea what you're talking about."

Of course there is no 119 North Weatherly, that lilting address that Mary recites on the show. The real house is a multi-million dollar, single-family dwelling at 2104 Kenwood Parkway. (What's in a name indeed!)

"Are you sure you're up for a walk like this?" Angie asks when we map the distance from our hotel to the landmark I've waited more than twenty years to see. "GPS says it's 2.8 miles each way."

"Let's do it!"

The air is brisk for April, and I'm thrilled to see my breath. I tell Angie how I wanted to apply to Carleton College as an undergrad, how eager I was to study in the Mary Richards city.

"So why didn't you?"

"My parents, you know. They were against me going anywhere out of state."

She stuffs her hands into her pockets. "I think your parents were against you going anywhere out of *sight*." Of course she's right.

We walk on together, and our bodies cast long shadows as the road ahead of us begins to rise. "You still good with this? I think it might be something of a climb."

I think but don't say—because I think it might be too saccharine to say—*everything worthwhile is.*

Before the fall, I could walk three miles in forty minutes, easy. I could walk three miles without thinking about it, three miles without chasing a breath. This time it takes two hours, and my ankle swells to boulder-size inside my shoe. I can feel the place where my leg is bolted back together—the tightness in the joint and the way the cold has climbed inside.

"I can call a taxi any time," Angie says. "Want me to download the Uber app?" When I shake my head, she intercedes, clasping my wrist with her hand: "I *really think* that's what Mary Richards would do."

But then before I can refuse her the house appears—all 9500 square feet, 7 bedrooms, and 6.5 baths of it—and no one is circling the block or congregating on the corner. No one is gawking and loitering but us. And on this quiet weekday afternoon, I ask Angie to take my picture from every angle, especially beside the FOR SALE sign.

"You could tell everyone back home you bought it, that you'll rent out the place for writing retreats and other special occasions."

And because Angie is a poet, too, she knows I'm invoking Adrienne Rich as I exclaim, jubilant despite the throbbing: "This is the thing I came for—the thing itself and not the myth!"

SEASON HIGHLIGHTS: AGE 36

When I am thirty-six, my beloved and I move into a high-rise apartment on the beach. We've been dreaming of a place like this since we first arrived in South Florida, and now, three years later, the rents are right, and a unit comes available just as our old lease expires.

At the new place, we can stroll out to a backyard of sand and surf. Our balcony faces the city lights, overlooks the Intracoastal Waterway. Far below us, cars glide past, pearlescent on the narrow string of Ocean Drive.

For thirteen years across four different states, we've lived in funky old houses converted to apartments that favor charm over modern convenience. We've had a single bedroom, a single bath, a fold-out couch in the living room for visitors. If they're friend enough to be staying with us they know I'm bound to mention Mary Richards as I stow the sofa cushions and produce a pair of pillows from behind the closet door.

The episode "Mary Moves Out" was written at the beginning of season six when the owners of the house at 2104 Kenwood Parkway grew weary of all the MTM fans loitering on their corner, driving by slowly and around the block again, posing for picture after picture outside their famous home. They posted IMPEACH NIXON signs in the yard and hung them from the now-iconic Palladian windows to prevent MTM camera crews from gathering new footage.

This practical need for updated exterior shots was channeled in more symbolic ways into Mary's character. Rhoda and Phyllis had both moved out and on in previous seasons, and as Georgette told Mary in her sweet, literal way, "If you move I might have to stop coming here all together." We don't know if Mary likes her new neighbors, but we know she must miss the camaraderie we all associate with that warm bright space, its high ceilings and low bookshelves, and the pleasing step down into her living room.

Angie and I were excited to try out the anonymity, or at least the greater privacy, of high-rise life. The hallways in our new building were so long and quiet, the appliances so new and shiny, and the glass was storm-resistant in every unit too—a luxury in coastal Florida.

There were other amenities as well, similar to those Mary raves about when she describes her new place to Mr. Grant. Our building had a pool, a sauna, a hot tub, a gym. It was more urban and contemporary than any place we had ever lived before.

I thought of Mary—how could I not?—when the movers had finished unloading our furniture and stacking our boxes inside the front door, when I could no longer hear the last hand truck rolling away. Angie was still at work that first day, so it was just me and our kitties, alone in the cavernous room, alone with the spectacular view.

Even without the IMPEACH NIXON signs, I reasoned, wasn't it time for Mary to enjoy a few perks of her middle-thirties—earning a little more, paying a little more, updating the interiors too? Like hers, our balcony faced other high-rises across the road, and I chuckled at the thought of Ted encouraging Mary to "sunbathe in the nude out there." When she resists, he counters, "So you'll do it at night!"

Yet despite everything favorable about the move, Mary confides to herself (we are merely eavesdropping now), "I don't like it." This is another way of saying, "I don't like change" and "This is going to take some getting used to." And while I'm sure we too are going to fall in love with our life at the beach, I sit down on the bare floor and feel—what is it exactly?—something poignant and imprecise.

Mary explains to Lou: "I felt this way about my old place when I moved from my old old place."

Then she hangs her letter, of course. Her friends come to take her out to dinner, but Mary tells them all to go ahead without her, that she'll catch up soon. That's when she takes the hammer, holds the nails in her teeth, and makes that first resolute mark on her new wall.

I don't have a J of my own—not even on a mug or a Christmas tree ornament—which strikes me as strange after all these years. Was Mary's M a gift? Why had no one ever thought to give me a J? But on further reflection, it seemed more likely that Mary made the M or bought it for herself as celebration or invocation of some personal milestone. Maybe I would make myself or buy myself a J when I got tenure—*if*.

For now, I reach into my satchel and take out the books that bear my name. Publishing is always a bit like moving into a new place, forging a new relationship with the work that once belonged to you and you alone. For all the exhilaration, there comes a moment like this one, a moment in a quiet room, just you and the letters you once put down on the page.

I make a crescent moon of my own volumes, touch their covers one by one. I have never written the book I thought I was writing, never the book I set out to write. This, too, is a poignant, imprecise feeling, but I remind myself that I have lettered after all.

SEASON HIGHLIGHTS: AGE 37

Linda B. sends me a birthday card with a bright thirty-seven on the cover. Inside she has written: "Here's to your milestone! Are you any closer to solving the mystery of what happens at the end of those Mary years?"

I write back: "This is my fifth year teaching in a tenure-track job, which forces the issue: either they decide to keep me, *permanently*, and I become an Associate Professor—sounds a lot like 'Associate Producer,' don't you think?—or they have to let me go."

Unlike Mary, who was fired without any warning, I've always known my day of reckoning would come, that my hiring at the university was provisional in terms far more carefully controlled and enforced than Mr. Grant's grumpy proviso: *If I don't like you, I'll fire you*. (But they do! I know they do!) *If I don't like you, I'll fire you!* (But I do! I have found, as they say, "my people"! I have found, as I say, my WJM at last!)

The tenure application process is slow and methodical, consuming most of the academic year. It requires me to provide extensive documentation of my publishing, teaching, and service over the last half-decade. As I scan poems and essays at the copy machine to create the requisite PDFs, I'm reminded of the girl I was at eleven, twelve, thirteen, hoarding her change to feed the great behemoth called Xerox in the back corner of the library. Though everything is uploaded now instead of collated with folders in three-ring binders, compiling a tenure file requires the same tenacity and comprehensiveness of a young fan building her archive.

On January 25, 2017, I am teaching my afternoon poetry course, followed by my evening multi-genre seminar. It's a precious time away from texts and emails, those eight hours of face-to-face and voice-to-voice exchange. But while I'm packing my bags to travel from one classroom to the next, I notice the red numbers climbing. There are sixteen texts so far, no make that eighteen, twenty. . . . I've either won a major literary prize, or someone I love has died. The thought is so clear I fear I have spoken it aloud.

I touch the screen and wait for the words to rise. *I'm so sorry* is all I see. Then I scan them. I search for my beloved's name. She has written too: *I just heard.* . . . Now I can breathe again, but I can't face the unknown, not yet. As I climb the stairs and greet my students, I'm thinking of Georgette at the passing of Chuckles the Clown: "Funerals always come too late." It was funny how she said it, but the sentiment was no less profound. I was late already, to whatever loss this was, and I would have to be a little later.

I remember, too, how I used the computer in class that night, which was uncharacteristic for me. There was a screen that slid down and a digital projector, and as I dimmed the lights and lowered the screen, one of the students exclaimed, "Movie time!"

There was a certain cinematic feeling to the space, and we were writing ekphrastically after all, writing in response to images. I had prepared a slideshow, but I encouraged my students to seek out images on their own that inspired them. "It doesn't have to be a well-known work of art like Monet's waterlilies or Degas' ballerinas," I said. "You can write in response to any visual text that moves you—paintings, photographs, film, even television."

"Can you give us an example?" someone asked.

"Sure." I nodded. A quick Google Image search, and there she was, on the big screen that spanned the width of our white board—Mary Tyler Moore as Mary Richards, tossing her tam high into the air, the iconic moment captured on film and then frozen in time.

"Does anyone recognize this image?" I asked. They weren't sure. They wanted to check their phones, but I wouldn't let them. "It's not a test," I said. "It's OK if you've never seen it before. Just tell me what you see. Better still: write it down."

My students looked younger on this night than usual—something about the screen-glow perhaps—and I wondered if I looked older—unfathomably old to them. Soon, I realized, I will have students born in the twenty-first century, with no recollection of any time at all before the new millennium. Unless they make a conscious practice of looking back, the 1970s will seem as far away and irrelevant to their lives as the Middle Ages.

"She looks jubilant," a young woman says about Mary.

"Did she just graduate or something?" a young man chimes in.

"There's a neon sign in the background, but I can't quite make out what it says. Maybe the Krispy Kreme doughnuts are hot, but I'm kind of doubting they had them back then."

"Is that what they mean by a pea coat?" This is Florida after all.

"She's older than you think, but she still has a youthful spirit."

"I think she looks like someone told her to just throw caution to the wind."

"She has a pom-pom on her hat. Is that significant?"

"The color scheme is almost patriotic, like they're trying to say something about an all-American girl."

"She looks Latina to me." This is Miami after all.

"She looks like she had a secret, and then she let it go. It's out of her hands now."

Cristian, in the back row, Cristian who never volunteers, raises his hand now. When I call on him, he says: "Prof, she looks like you."

The room grows quiet as they regard me, and I in turn regard the image: Mary, me, juxtaposed. A few of the other students concur.

I tell them to go home and write their stories, their poems, their personal essays inspired by something they have seen. Keats had his Grecian urn, and Carole Maso had Frida Kahlo, and Mark Doty had the Dutch still-lifes (or are they *still-lives*, which makes me think of that which is still living), and Brenda Miller had Edward Weston's photograph that became the cover of her book, and Rick Barot had the Madonna holding the child who in turn was holding a tuber fresh from the earth.

"There is no telling," I tell them, "what might inspire you. But once you find it, make your reader see it too—make sure we *feel* it."

"And can we write about her if we want?" Audree asks, pointing to the screen—"you know, *ekphrastically?*" I nod. "Great! There's something like old-timey about her but also appealing. I was thinking she could even be a vampire or something!"

When everyone has left the room, I am still standing in front of the screen in semi-darkness. We're the last class of the night, and the building empties quickly. Sometimes it's creepy. Sometimes it's peaceful. Tonight it's hard to tell which.

I reach for my phone, knowing I must face the loss at hand now: *Forty-eight messages, fifty. There are voicemails too.*

I click the first text, which is the most recent in a long row:

She was a legend and a comic genius. You were the first person I thought of when I read she had passed.

And there it was:

RIP MTM.

My hand finds its way to my heart again.

She turned the world on with her smile, and you do too. Thinking of you tonight.

I look over my shoulder, and she's still there: Mary, full-screen; Mary, indelible.

Linda wrote:

You have my deepest sympathies. She was an inspiration to many people, but she passed you a special torch, and you've carried it all these years.

How could I bring myself to turn off the screen now, to power down like the laminated instructions insisted I should?

She was 80. That's a long, good life, especially for someone with diabetes. Still, I know this fact doesn't make it any easier to lose your heroine. I don't like to think of a world without Mary Tyler Moore in it.

So I leave the screen on, knowing that later tonight someone will come into this room—to clean it perhaps—and will flip the switch that turns everything dark, quiets the hum from the high projector.

I knew you'd be teaching today, and I thought that maybe that's for the best. Mary found her calling in television news, and you found your calling writing and teaching. The classroom is your WJM.

But whoever comes, I hope that person will catch a glimpse of Mary, perhaps remember her from another time or simply remember her hereafter.

April wrote:

Oh, Julie. It breaks my heart, as I know it breaks yours. This was never the ending we could have imagined for your Mary Richards' years.

And I don't know how it took me so long—a quarter-century is no brief spell—but when I saw "Richards" there at the end of her name, I recognized for the first time the implicit tribute to Mary's real-life son. *Of course!* She kept her name as the character's first name, and she took Richard, her son's name, and made it the last. Mary Richards was another way of carrying him with her every day into the role she played.

DIRECTOR'S NOTE: Tonight a thirty-seven-year-old woman opens the moon roof in her Honda CRV and lets a well-known theme song pour its full-pitched elegy into the clear Miami night. The woman is not praying, but as she drives north on Biscayne Boulevard, she imagines Mary in the seat beside her, riding shotgun to her very own story. She may thank her. She may even speak the words of gratitude aloud. If she had a hat, she'd toss it through the open portal over her head, but this is Florida after all, where it is never cold, so she tosses a brightly colored kerchief instead.

SERiES fiNALE

When the final episode of *The Mary Tyler Moore Show* aired, our eponymous star was forty years old. She had, without knowing it, exactly half her life left to live.

I marvel as I think about it now: what we most often celebrate of Mary Tyler Moore comes from the first half of her life. Ahead were so many new starting lines, critical acclaim in dramatic roles—the film *Ordinary People*, the Broadway play *Whose Life Is it Anyway*. She would dance with the Russian ballet. She would travel to Rome with her mother and have a private audience with the Pope. And yes, her marriage was going to end and her son was going to die, but she was also going to find love again in her forties and spend the rest of her life with the person who saw her most clearly.

Robert Levine once said in an interview that he remembered watching *The Dick Van Dyke Show* as a kid and having a crush on Laura Petrie. Of course he never dreamed he would grow up to marry the woman who had portrayed her. Life is funny that way. I too remembered watching *The Dick Van Dyke Show* as a kid and the great relief it was *not* to have a crush on Laura Petrie. But maybe, just maybe, I would let the walnuts spill from my own closet someday. I would find the sparkling one that held my own strange and mysterious power. Then I would put on my Capri pants and dance with abandon.

The night Mary Tyler Moore died, I went home to my high-rise apartment and watched with my beloved Episode 168, aptly titled "The Last Show." Rhoda and Phyllis return to comfort Mary as she prepares to produce her final show for WJM.

The cast rehearsed all week delivering their lines without emotion so that, on the night of the live taping, their tears would be real, not forced. The actors wept through into their parts. Is it Lou Grant who murmurs "I treasure you people," or is it Ed Asner, or both? Two men visible in one body. And of course, there is Mary—MR, MTM—alone in the newsroom one last time. She's making a memory of this moment, of this workplace that both the character and the actor have shared for seven years. No script is needed anymore.

In a few months, at the tail end of my thirty-seventh year, I will upload and submit a completed tenure portfolio: many PDFs, more than a thousand pages in all. Then I will wait. *What happens next?* I won't know the answer until my Mary years are over, until the next season of my life has begun.

Recently the dean's office added an opportunity for faculty members under consideration for tenure to stand before their departments and speak briefly on their own behalf. Here's what Mary said to her colleagues on the final episode, words I find are no less true for me, even as a married woman. Family is capacious after all. Family is more capacious than a closet can ever be:

Well, I just wanted you to know that sometimes I
get concerned about being a career woman. I get
to thinking my job is too important to me, and I
tell myself that the people I work with are just
the people I work with and not my family. And
last night I thought, What is a family anyway?
They're just people who make you feel less alone
and really loved. And that's what you've done for
me. Thank you for being my family.

But I won't speak these words out loud. Instead I will hold them in my throat as I type my full name into the box to "certify that everything I have presented here is true, to the best of my awareness and without any intention to deceive":

 X   Julie Marie Wade

Three names, five syllables, fourteen letters. We become ourselves through other people after all.

closing credits

closing credits

I was smiling when it began, hamming it up in all my baby pictures. The shift happens slowly. A melancholy tinge appears around the edges of old photographs, the white borders where they write in the names. There's something called "Throwback Thursday" now. We post pictures of earlier selves, earlier lives on Facebook. Like this one: I'm five years old, just fitted for my first glasses, and I clutch the book in my hand like a raft, like I've been drowning or like I expect to be. Then I'm downcast in the fancy dresses, paraded around by my mother in the neighborhood fashion show. My eyes are closed in all the pictures at Bible School. Then I'm Velma from *Scooby-Doo* for Halloween, in the orange turtleneck sweater with a magnifying glass. April is Daphne. Our smiles are real.

I'm a character in search of a script until I put on a pair of my mother's bell-bottom jeans, the faded pink shirt with the beaded peacock, a rainbow head scarf. Then I'm Rhoda. I'm happy. I'm making somebody laugh. Or I'm Mary with my hair bobbed and a polyester shirt from a thrift store that cinches at the waist with little red buttons all the way down. Later I'm on a date with a man, then another man, and I'm trying to smile, but you can see the hesitation at the corners of my mouth. I'm fitting somebody for a shoe at the store, and I like the idea of being the Prince so much more than being Cinderella. Then there's a wedding dress in the back of the car, a bit of the white skirt dragging. I'm smiling because I skipped out. I'm smiling because Angie is driving, and no one is watching too close as we sail off into the sunrise—east toward new starting lines. But later I'm weeping on a therapist's couch, where no one takes a picture, where no one would ever dare. I'm telling him that most people don't have to give up their parents when they find true love, exchange one family for another. He wants me to "take a good look at myself in the mirror." I watch *The Mary Tyler Moore Show* instead. He wants me to "make peace with the parts of my past I can neither change nor reclaim." I write about *The Mary Tyler Moore Show* for a TV analysis class. He wants me to contemplate—not to force, but to contemplate—the idea of closure. Then my Aunt Linda dies. Then my Grandma June dies. Funerals come too late, but there are no funerals for them. My parents move south to another state, start a new life in the face of the shame I have wrought. Yet here I am smiling at my students as they read their poems aloud. It is not forced. Here I am smiling with my whole face and also my eyes the day Angie and I stand before a make-shift altar in The Black Cat restaurant and bar. And here I am even smiling in the ER with my leg in a cast. Someone comments: "You're resilient! You'll bounce back!" And here I am, one early morning in Minneapolis, when the April rain is turning to snow, and I haven't run anywhere in almost six months. I put my uneasy foot into my new running shoe, lace it myself. The ankle is swollen still, but the shoe fits well enough, and then I'm running, and Angie is running beside me, and this time we won't stop until we reach the statue they've erected in her honor, until I am standing breathless at her bronze feet while Angie snaps the picture. These are my Mary years after all, and I'm smiling like I have some idea where I'm going.

acknowledgments

"Opening Credits" (published as "Our Lady of the Smile"), *North American Review*, 2020.

"Time Capsule/Snow Globe" (published as "Origin Story"), *North American Review*, 2020.

"Fauntlee Hills Was My Roseburg" (published as "Fauntlee Hills Was My Roseburg: An Essay in Episodes"), *Prairie Schooner*, 2020.

"Lamonts Might Be My WJM" (published as "Lamonts Was My WJM: An Essay in Episodes"), *Grist*, 2019.

"Pittsburgh Was My Minneapolis" (published as "Pittsburgh Was My Minneapolis: An Essay in Episodes"), *Tupelo Quarterly*, 2018.

"Miami Is My Tipperary" (published as "Miami Is My Tipperary: An Essay in Episodes"), *The Normal School*, 2020.

"Closing Credits" (published as "After All"), *North American Review*, 2020.

GRATITUDE

I am profoundly grateful to Michael Martone for selecting *The Mary Years* as the 2023 winner of the Clay Reynolds Novella Prize. That gratitude extends to Peter "PJ" Carlisle, Karisma "Charlie" Tobin, and the entire team at Texas Review Press for shepherding this collection to press and for embracing my unconventional project with a spirit of joyful innovation.

Thank you to my generous blurbers for their time and insights as well as their own inspiring work—Susanne Paola Antonetta, Heidi Czerwiec, Lee Ann Roripaugh, and Clifford Thompson.

Thank you to my sister-in-law Kim Striegel for taking my author photo in front of the 80s Disco Club in Dania Beach and for creating the JMW logo for this book, which features Tina, one of my two beautiful cats. (Kudos—and Greenies—to Beaufort as well.)

Since I was twenty-six, I've written a meditation essay almost every year. When I was thirty-seven, I tried to write a meditation essay about the end of my "Mary years," which grew and grew until it became a book. In many ways I've been writing this book since I was twelve years old, the year I sent my first fan letter to Mary Tyler Moore. Signing off on these galleys at age forty-five, I realize this is *still* my fan letter to you, Mary— an elegy for your remarkable life and an homage to how I've learned, and continue learning, from it.

As it turns out, my life has been full of Marys. I'm thankful for each of them, and also for you, dear reader, for accompanying me all the way to this page. Thank you, April Davis and Linda Breuer, for sharing and shaping my youth with gentleness, honesty, and wisdom.

171

Thank you to all my incomparable teachers, especially David Seal, Dana Anderson, Tom Campbell, Brenda Miller, Bruce Beasley, Susanne Paola Antonetta, Annette Allen (rest in poetry), and Cate Fosl, who turned the world on with their luminous guidance.

Thank you to my enduring friends, especially Anna Rhodes and James Allen Hall, who have always tossed all my figurative tams with me.

Thank you to the singular Jan Becker for the gift of a *literal* Mary Richards tam. I keep it between my writing desk and my autographed picture of Mary Tyler Moore—and whenever I travel somewhere cold enough to wear it, I always do.

Thank you to my "Outlaws"—Kim and Matt Striegel—and my niblings, Evie, Nolan, and Sam—for your love and acceptance these last twenty-two years. I am so fortunate to call you my family.

Thank you to all the women I worked with at Lamonts in Westwood Village from 1997-2000. You may never know how much you taught me, but I know I will never forget.

Thank you to the Marys of Pittsburgh—especially Amy Patterson, Robin Godfrey, Connie Angermeier, and John H. Miller—to the Marys of Louisville—especially Carol Stewart, Elijah Pritchett, Amy Tudor, Rev Culver, Sara Northerner, James Leary, and Monica Krupinski—and to the Marys of Miami—especially Denise Duhamel, John Dufresne, Cindy Chinelly, Debra Dean, and Maureen Seaton (rest in poetry), and all my students and colleagues at Florida International University, who continue to remind me that love is all around.

Thank you most to Angie Griffin, my partner, spouse, and favorite person, with whom I have never spent a nothing day.